Now More Than Ever

Harry Ransom Humanities Research Center Imprint Series
Published from the Collection of the HRHRC

Reflections on James Joyce: Stuart Gilbert's Paris Journal,
edited by Thomas F. Staley and Randolf Lewis

The Letters of Ezra Pound to Alice Corbin Henderson,
edited by Ira B. Nadel

The Diaries of Nikolay Punin, 1904-1953,
edited by Sidney Monas and Jennifer Greene Krupala,
translated by Jennifer Greene Krupala

Now More Than Ever

by

ALDOUS
HUXLEY

Edited with an Introduction by
David Bradshaw
and James Sexton

University of Texas Press, Austin

Requests for permission to reproduce material from this work should
be sent to Permissions, University of Texas Press, P.O. Box 7819,
Austin, TX 78713-7819.

⊛ The paper used in this book meets the minimum requirements of
ANSI/NISO Z39.48-1992 (R1997) (Permanence of Paper).

Library of Congress Cataloging-in-Publication Data
Huxley, Aldous, 1894-1963.
Now more than ever / by Aldous Huxley ; edited by
David Bradshaw and James Sexton.
p.   cm. — (Harry Ransom Humanities Research Center
imprint series)
ISBN: 978-0-292-72866-0
1. Capitalists and financiers—Great Britain—Drama.
2. Fathers and daughters—Great Britain—Drama.
3. Communists—Great Britain—Drama.   I. Bradshaw, David.
II. Sexton, James.   III. Title.   IV. Series.
PR6015.U9 N68   2000
822'.912—dc21
99-058286

For Barbara and Janice

Contents

Acknowledgments

Copyright in Aldous Huxley's published and unpublished writings is owned by the Aldous L. Huxley Estate. The editors are grateful for permission to quote from this material, and, in particular, they would like to thank the literary executor of the estate, Dorris Halsey, for her advice and support.

We should also like to thank Cathy Henderson and her colleagues at the Harry Ransom Humanities Research Center for their unfailingly courteous and efficient help and advice, and Jim Burr and his colleagues at the University of Texas Press for their friendly, professional, and patient guidance.

James Sexton would like to thank the Social Sciences and Humanities Research Council of Canada for the generous assistance it has afforded him with this project.

Introduction

Though it was an ambition which was destined to remain unfulfilled at his death in 1963, the prospect of authoring a theatrical smash hit tantalized Aldous Huxley throughout his creative life. "Plays are obviously the things one must pay attention to," he told his brother Julian as early as July 1918. "Imprimis, they are the only literary essays out of which a lot of money can be made; and I am determined to make writing pay."[1] By 23 June 1920, in a letter to his father, Huxley had fixed even more firmly on popular drama as a means of escaping from what had by then become a "hectic life of activity . . . There is nothing but a commercial success that can free one from this deadly hustle. I shall go on producing plays till I can get one staged and successful."[2] As his life wore on, however, a "commercial success" on the stage was to prove ever more elusive. Yet over forty years later, on 17 November 1963, with just five days to live and too weak to hold a pen, Huxley dictated a letter to his literary agent in London informing him of "a new interest in a theatrical production of *After Many a Summer* [his seventh novel, published in 1939]. I will let you know whatever progress is made over here."[3] Although he had earned practically nothing from his plays over the past four decades, Huxley's enthusiasm for the medium had never flagged and even his imminent death seems not to have dampened his fervent hope of achieving success on the stage.

Widely believed to be "lost"[4] and scarcely "commercial" in its style and subject matter, *Now More Than Ever* represents Huxley's most substantial and absorbing work as a dramatist, with the possible exception of *The World of Light* (1931). It is a play that will surprise those inclined to associate the younger Huxley solely with an attitude of cynical detachment. The sincerity of *Now More Than Ever* is palpable, and readers of the play cannot fail to register the political engagement and ethical *gravitas* with which it is freighted. But while *Now More Than Ever* is undoubtedly a significant addition to Huxley's oeuvre, the most likely reason why he failed to get the play produced is equally clear:

it relies too obtrusively on the explication of ideas and opinions, and draws too sparingly on the components and conventions of the interwar well-made play. The expository set-pieces, which for Huxley were the backbone of his play, also vitiated the drama by slowing it down. Despite the drawing power of its famous author, the play must have seemed too great a risk to the producers and impresarios who read it in the early 1930s. Ultimately, it is a play more suited to the page than the stage: the epilogue is too protracted—and arguably superfluous—while the dialogue generally lacks sufficient nip and punch. *Now More Than Ever* was unquestionably topical, but too untypical of its time to deliver the packed auditoria Huxley craved.

A partial explanation of why Huxley made so few concessions to the demands of the commercial theatre is provided, perhaps, in a comment he made during the course of an interview which took place in January 1931. "My chief motive in writing," Huxley remarked:

> has been the desire to clarify a point of view. Or, rather, the desire to clarify a point of view to myself. I do not write for my readers; in fact, I don't like thinking about my readers . . . I am chiefly interested in making clear a certain outlook on life . . . My books represent different stages in my progress towards such an outlook. Each book is an attempt to make things clear to myself so far as I had gone at the time it was written. In that sense they are all provisional . . . I believe that mankind is working towards some definite and comprehensive outlook on the world, and I regard my work as contributing something towards that.[5]

While it is impossible to square Huxley's "chief motive in writing" *Now More Than Ever* with his desire to write a box-office blockbuster, this play, like *Brave New World* (1932), the text which immediately preceded it, may be understood as part and parcel of Huxley's anxious "clarif[ication]" of his response to the social, economic, and political upheavals of the late 1920s and the early 1930s,[6] and, even more strikingly, as an integral part of his concerted effort to "clarify" himself to himself. Through the character of Walter Clough in particular, *Now More Than Ever* attests to Huxley's rejection of the hard line elitist ideology which had shored up his writing prior to and (more debatably) including *Brave New World*, and it bears intriguing witness to Huxley's search for a more humanitarian, down-to-earth, and "comprehensive outlook on the world." Like the Swiss scientist and balloonist Auguste Piccard (1884–1962), who with his brother Jean-Félix reached a record-breaking altitude of 16,940 meters in 1932, Huxley thought of himself as "extraordinarily cut off from people and things" at this time,[7] and in the three years which followed the writing of *Now More Than Ever* he experimented with breathing exercises, the Hay Diet, the Alexander Technique, and other reconstructive regimes, before concluding the overhaul of his body and mind by committing himself to absolute pacifism in November 1935. Clough's attacks on Philip Barmby's outlook and lifestyle in *Now More Than Ever* are the kind of criticisms which Huxley leveled against himself during this period. Indeed, Clough, Arthur Lidgate, his daughter Joan, and especially Barmby, with his "famous cynicism" and "hermetically sealed" ductless glands, all find themselves wanting in ways which mirror Huxley's profound dissatisfaction with his own life and work in the early 1930s. As Joan puts it at one point: "Why does one always have to be oneself?" Like Barmby, Huxley was increasingly disposed to regard himself as "just a dilettante with a gift of the gab." Joan accuses Barmby of being "so resigned" and sad, so stuck in a groove, just as Huxley himself felt stuck and dissatisfied with the role which had made him famous in the 1920s, the role of detached and insouciant cynic. He was desperate to commit himself to a cause, in the same way that Clough has devoted himself to communism, but in 1932 he had scant idea what that cause might be.

The decade which concluded with Huxley domiciled in California and attempting (with mixed results) to write for the movies began with him having his early interest in the theatre rekindled. In January 1930 he attended the final rehearsals of *This Way to Paradise*, Campbell Dixon's adaptation of *Point Counter Point* (1928), and he plainly found the experience inspiring:

> Mr. Dixon has given me an opportunity of vicariously tasting the joys and sorrows of the dramatist's life. The sip has been disquieting but heady. I am tempted, in spite of my unshakable affection for the novel, to renew the draught.[8]

By this point in his career, in addition to his novels, short stories, and nonfictional work, Huxley had written three plays,[9] two short parodies of John Drinkwater's historical dramas,[10] and three dramatic sketches.[11] One of Huxley's plays, *Happy Families,* had been performed (in his presence) at Harold Scott's and Elsa Lanchester's Cave of Harmony nightclub,[12] while his adaptation of *The Discovery* (1763) by Frances Sheridan was staged by Nigel Playfair at the Lyric Theatre, Hammersmith, London, in 1924.[13]

Following his stimulating visit to the rehearsals of *This Way to Paradise,* Huxley sat down to write for the stage once more and the result was *The World of Light.* In essence a satire on spiritualism, this play, like all Huxley's writings in the 1930s, prompted him to engage in a kind of psychological stocktaking. As he was to do again in *Eyeless in Gaza* (1936), Huxley explores his predominantly hostile feelings toward his father in *The World of Light.* Like Mr. Wenham in the play, Leonard Huxley, following the death, in 1908, of his first wife Julia (Aldous's mother), had married, in 1912, a much younger woman, Rosalind Bruce, and had subsequently had two children with her— and both the novel and the play depict, *inter alia,* a son's aversion to paternal attempts at affection. Interestingly, the son, Hugo Wenham, is a desiccated, disillusioned, and Barmby-like cynic of thirty, who even regards himself as "A dead vacuum." [14]

The World of Light opened at London's Royalty Theatre on 30 March 1931, but although Desmond MacCarthy reviewed it enthusiastically—"Encore! Mr. Huxley, more, please more!" [15]—other critics were less impressed with the play and it closed before the end of its scheduled run. Undeterred, its producer, Leon M. Lion, urged Huxley to continue writing for the theatre, suggesting that he might, for example, attempt an adaptation of his much-discussed *Brave New World.*[16] Huxley rejected this idea but he did not turn his back on the stage, and in July 1932 he informed his literary agent that he was

> working on the scenario of what may be, I think, rather a good play—with a Kreuger-like figure as the central character—linking the story up with general economic ideas, which might be timely, as everyone is bothered about these things.[17]

Huxley and his contemporaries were undoubtedly deeply "bothered" by the extraordinary revelations which followed the suicide of the Swedish financier Ivar Kreuger in Paris in March 1932. Prior to his death, the wealth and power of "The Match King"—Kreuger's sobriquet derived from his monopoly of global production—were legendary, but it soon became apparent that Kreuger's assets largely consisted of bogus bonds, chimerical companies, and cooked accounts. The impact of this bombshell on "general economic ideas" was considerable, and the sheer scale of Kreuger's fraud led to his posthumous installation as "the greatest swindler the world had ever known."[18] In the eyes of many intellectuals, especially those on the left, Kreuger came to embody the chicanery, deceit, and malfeasance at the heart of free-market capitalism. Two years earlier, the novelist Richard Aldington had caught the tenor of the time when he addressed the disillusionment of "the younger generation" in his review of Evelyn Waugh's *Vile Bodies* (1930):

> They were ushered into life during one of the meanest and most fraudulent decades staining the annals of history. And it's still going on—forgery, fraudulent bankruptcy, false banknotes, intensive commercial welfare, lying conferences to deceive the nations' demand for peace . . .[19]

As well as being the primary model for *Now More Than Ever*'s Arthur Lidgate—who knows that after his death he will be revealed as "one of the biggest swindlers on record"—Kreuger was also the original of Erik Krogh in *England Made Me* (1935),[20] the novel which Graham Greene set against the "sense of capitalism staggering from crisis to crisis."[21]

On 27 August 1932, Huxley provided Lion with a more detailed synopsis of his current project:

> I am writing a politico-economic play more or less about Kreuger; i.e. a financier with a sincere desire to rationalize the world, but who bites off more than he can chew and is driven into swindling and finally suicide. His daughter falls in love with a young man who has given up his social position to preach communism—and he with her; but he refuses to allow himself to love

this incarnation of the luxuries and drives her off with a get-thee-behind-me-Satan gesture, until, at the end, the father's sins and suicide make a union possible. Add to this a secretary to the financier—a profound sceptic who riddles both sides with his criticisms and himself enjoys the comfort of a cynical conformity to things as they are. One or two minor characters, and there you are. I have written an act and a half, and hope to get ahead in the next few weeks. There will be a good deal of talk—but on subjects in which everybody is now interested.[22]

In the circumstances, Huxley's description of Kreuger as "a financier with a sincere desire to rationalize the world" seems excessively permissive if not perverse. Yet this representation of Kreuger as a noble-spirited altruist is one which was quite common at the time. One commentator wrote:

His early achievements as a builder who brought new methods and created new values are of lasting merit. The same applies to the trustification and modernisation of the match industry. On these scores alone he deserves different consideration than an inveterate swindler pure and simple. Furthermore, the loans he made were definitely constructive and helped the rehabilitation of a number of countries [following the Wall Street Crash of 1929]. He may have raised the money in a dishonest way, but he used at least a part of it in a way that was beneficial to the world. His match loans were not only based on most solid foundations; they also contributed to peace and stability.[23]

Another contemporary, Raymond Poincaré, prime minister and finance minister of France from 1926 to 1929, called Kreuger "An outstanding and honest man of unusually well developed and balanced gifts," and the distinguished economist J. M. Keynes, a friend of Huxley's in the early 1930s and someone with whom he no doubt discussed the Swedish financier's life and untimely death, portrayed an equally sympathetic figure in his radio obituary of 14 March 1932:

In Ivar Kreuger's death we have just seen a moving example of the helplessness of the individual. Here we had a man who possessed what was perhaps the greatest constructive financial talent of his era, a man whose wide-embracing activity in the most comprehensive sense of the term was of general significance and who regarded it as his task to create, in the postwar chaos, channels between countries with capital resources in abundance and those in bitter need of these. He built upon solid ground and secured his work with all the guarantees that lay in human power to devise. He lived to experience what the ignorant would call the usual fate of the gambler, but in reality Ivar Kreuger was crushed between icebergs of a frozen world, which is not within human power to thaw out and give the warmth of normal life.[24]

Huxley continued to work on *Now More Than Ever* throughout September 1932. He was also reading *War and Peace* at this time, "which, I find, is a great consolation and tonic," he told a correspondent on 1 October. "In the intervals I try to write a play—which is interesting and difficult."[25] By 10 October, however, he was able to inform his literary agent, J. Ralph Pinker (who was himself to be jailed for swindling his clients, including Huxley, a few years later) that he had completed his task:

I have finished my play and will send it to you in a few days, when I have done the typing. I read it to some friends yesterday and the effect was good; which is encouraging.

I know you have certain objections to Lion. But I feel under considerable obligation to him for having cheerfully lost money on two of my efforts [as well as *The World of Light*, Lion also promoted *This Way to Paradise*]; and I want him to have the first opportunity of losing more—or recouping his losses—on this one. The one condition must be, I think: *not* in matinées. For I'm convinced that did a lot of harm to *The World of Light*.[26]

"Let's hope a few members of the theatre going public may find it as interesting as I do," he told another correspondent. "They didn't go near my other play."[27] Huxley sent a copy of *Now More Than Ever* to the London-based writer and translator Sydney Schiff (who wrote under the *nom de plume* of "Stephen Hudson") on 3 November,[28] and the following month he, too, arrived in London from his home on the French Riviera, informing an interviewer:

I'm in London because I've written a new play. It's called *Now More Than Ever* and it deals with the subject of a man like Kreuger or Hatry. I suppose it really might be called a study of the present-day financial and economic position of the world.[29]

Huxley had linked Kreuger with Clarence Hatry, the leading figure in an enormous City of London Stock Exchange fraud of 1929, earlier in 1932 when he made his first published comment on Kreuger's suicide.[30] In quoting what Huxley wrote on that occasion, it is worth underlining the affinity between his benevolent attitude to Kreuger and Keynes's equally benign spin on the financier's activities:

> Business, the reformers tell us, and after business, government, must be organised in ever larger and larger units. Kreuger was profoundly convinced of this; so was Hatry. Both men, I imagine, were, among other things, far-sighted idealists. In attempting to act on their enlightened convictions, to put their sociological ideals into practice, both were forced into gigantic fraud.[31]

"It is a play I shall be proud to stage," Lion had written to Huxley after reading *The World of Light*, "though I dare not flatter you or myself that it will make an appeal to more than a limited public. It is a *thinker's* play which in the old days the Stage Society would have done."[32] This was a perceptive comment, and in his review of the play the critic Ashley Dukes had even predicted that *The World of Light* "may prove to be the *Widowers' Houses* of some new revival of intellectual drama."[33] But this had not happened, and one can imagine how crestfallen the commercially minded Lion must have felt when he first read *Now More Than Ever*, even though he had been warned to expect "a good deal of talk." In the event, it was clearly too much of "a *thinker's* play" even for Lion, who, had he been familiar with them, might have felt inclined to redirect toward their author Huxley's comments on John Galsworthy's *Plays: Fourth Series*:

> [T]he literature of social problems . . . possesses life and value only in so far as its characters are real, individual human beings. The problem does not make the play; it is the characters that cause us to be interested in or tolerant of the problem.[34]

Now More Than Ever's characters are not lifeless by any means, but they are insufficiently realized to allow Huxley to focus on his "problem" to the extent to which he does. Moreover, in his role as drama critic for the *Westminster Gazette*, Huxley had in 1920 reviewed a performance of Israel Zangwill's *The Melting Pot* (1909), and it could be argued that his critique of Zangwill's play is even more applicable to *Now More Than Ever* than his comments on Galsworthy's drama:

> The unsatisfactoriness of *The Melting Pot* naturally makes one think of the unsatisfactoriness of most of the so-called "drama of ideas." The drama is a form in which it is almost impossible to convey ideas of any complexity. To be understood at a first hearing by a mixed crowd of several hundred people an idea must be extraordinarily simple, and even then it must be repeated almost *ad nauseam* if it is to be thoroughly comprehended. Ideas of the least subtlety or novelty, controversial, difficult, obscure ideas simply escape a listening audience . . . [T]he difficulty of conveying an idea dramatically is so great, and the range of ideas that can be conveyed so limited, that one wonders why people who are interested in theories go to the trouble of writing a play when their notions could be far more subtly, accurately, and truly expressed in a novel or an essay.[35]

But even though Huxley was fully conversant with the pitfalls of the "drama of ideas," he did not possess the play-writing skills to negotiate them. Some years later, Beth Wendell, who worked with Huxley on a dramatization of his novel *The Genius and the Goddess* (1955), made the revealing observation that Huxley was "quite unable to visualize creatively . . . In order to imagine the projection of a play onto the stage, he needed to have it described by someone else. An important task of the collaborator was to supply all the descriptions of sets, action, entrances and exits." [36]

Although Huxley's attempts to get *Now More Than Ever* produced in London were unsuccessful, when he was in the United States in May 1933 he made some promising contacts and asked his agent to send him a copy of the play:

There are several people in New York interested in it, and I want to make some improvements in the first act—where several defects were pointed out to me by Miss [Theresa] Helburn [executive director] of the [New York Theatre] Guild.[37]

By June 1933, Huxley was back at home in the south of France, where he worked on a "revised version" of the play,[38] and it is almost certain that this is the revised and corrected typescript now held by the Harry Ransom Humanities Research Center at the University of Texas at Austin, on which the present edition of the play is based. Huxley's revisions, apart from rearranging the sequence of events in act I, largely consisted of unimportant alterations to the dialogue of his play, and they did not change its shape, substance, or style. Not surprisingly, therefore, he remained unable to find anyone willing to stage it. On 22 June 1934 he wrote rather plaintively to his literary agent: "I'm still waiting for Miss Helburn to come forward with her suggestion, but she seems to be otherwise occupied." [39]

Huxley persisted in his efforts to find a producer, and as late as December 1934 his literary agent was once again alerted to a possible production of his play, this time in London:

I met last night the man who runs the Shilling Theatre at Fulham [i.e., Robert Newton]. He expressed a desire to look at *Now More Than Ever*, and I think it would be a good idea to send him a copy . . . I should like to see some sort of performance of it, if only to be able to judge what should be done in the way of altering it—and I think he might quite possibly give it a show.[40]

Unfortunately for Huxley, the Shilling Theatre was forced to close for financial reasons soon after this meeting with Newton. Equally frustrating, no doubt, was a lunch at the Cheshire Cheese public house in London with Rupert Doone, Robert Medley, and other members of the experimental Group Theatre. "The possibility of a play by [Huxley] was of course the reason for the party, which was a very enjoyable one, but nothing came of it," Medley recalled in 1984.[41] And unsurprisingly: in comparison with the "distinctly new wave"[42] of drama which comprised the Group Theatre's repertoire, *Now More Than Ever* would have seemed distinctly passé to the likes of Doone and Medley. Huxley abandoned his play soon afterward and concentrated on making progress with *Eyeless in Gaza*. *Now More Than Ever* was eventually performed (before its editors, if not its author) at the University of Münster, Germany, on 27 June 1994, as part of the University's "Aldous Huxley Centenary Symposium"—the first of six performances staged during the symposium by the English department's drama group.

If the two most obvious "social problems" with which *Now More Than Ever* is concerned are the scandal of economic muddle and the wickedness of financial speculation, the topical issues from which it derives its impetus, in addition to Krueger's suicide, are the vogue for corporate planning in the early 1930s and the simultaneous campaign for the wholesale rationalization of Britain's industrial base. Huxley was a vehement proponent of national planning, declaring in May 1931, for instance, "We must either plan or else go under,"[43] while in September 1932, in the midst of writing *Now More Than Ever,* he published an article in which he observed:

> A growing body of public opinion is now in favor of the deliberate planning of our social life in all its aspects. It is an ideal which must, it seems to me, appeal to every reasonable man. Viewing the chaos to which a planless individualism has reduced us, we are compelled to be believers in planning.[44]

Planning, indeed, was something of a family passion. In *If I Were Dictator* (1934), Julian Huxley argued that "the conscious and scientific planning of society" was no less than "the fourth great step in human history."[45]

Rationalization had become a buzz word of the late 1920s following the League of Nations's World Economic Conference in Geneva in May 1927. The conference's Industrial Committee produced a number of resolutions under the general heading of "Rationalisation" which were adopted by the conference as a whole. These recommended "that Governments, public institutions, professional and industrial organisations, and the general public should . . . diffuse in every quarter a clear understanding of the advantages and obligations involved by Rationalisation and Scientific Management, and of the possibilities of their gradual application."[46] Another contemporary commentator, Sir Mark Webster Jenkinson, defined rationalization as:

> . . . the fusion of manufacturing capacity and the closing down of redundant units to eliminate waste and loss, production being concentrated in the best equipped shops under the most favourable output conditions. It involves not merely a reconstruction of capital, a reorganisation of management, a re-shuffling of plant, but a revolution in our ideas, in our mentality, in our outlook on the industrial situation.[47]

As Britain attempted to come to terms with increasing industrial competition not only from the likes of Germany and the United States, but also from France, Italy, and Japan, it was widely believed that she must either reform her manufacturing base and coordinate her national effort, or else she would go to the wall. The vogue for rationalization in Britain was synonymous with Sir Alfred Mond, Lord Melchett (1868–1930), who had amalgamated the diffuse British chemical industry into the giant Imperial Chemical Industries Limited (ICI) in 1926. In February 1931, Huxley toured the vast ICI chemicals plant at Billingham in the northeast of England and acclaimed it as "one of those ordered universes that exist as anomalous oases of pure logic in the midst of the larger world of planless incoherence," and in *Brave New World*, which he wrote soon afterwards, Huxley gives the name Mond to the Resident World Controller for Western Europe.[48]

In *Jesting Pilate* (1926), Huxley condemns financial speculation as "the most discreditable, unproductive and socially mischievous" way of making money,[49] and in 1933 he predicted that "In the planned economy, which the rulers of almost every civilized country are now trying to impose, there will be no room for speculation in stocks."[50] The bursting of Wall Street's speculative bubble in 1929, coupled with the Hatry and Kreuger scandals, deeply perturbed Huxley not least because of the Italian economist and sociologist Vilfredo Pareto's singling out of speculators as figures who

> rejoice in dangerous economic ventures and are on the watch for them. In appearance they are always submissive to the man who shows himself the stronger; but they work underground

an excellent book on the present economic situation—*The Economic Consequences of Power Production,* by Fred Henderson ... which I greatly recommend you to read if you have the chance. I am sure he has got hold of the essential inwardness of the situation. But, alas, it takes a fearful long time for such books to make any effect on governments. "In politics, everything is as stupid as it seems." Bagehot, I think—and painfully true![59]

As its title suggests, Henderson's study addresses the grievous overproduction inherent in highly mechanized economies, and it helped to reinforce Huxley's fears about the social and strategic perils of the unplanned state.

But if *Now More Than Ever* is largely shaped and driven by Huxley's concern with macroeconomic problems in the 1930s, the extra stimulus it acquired from Huxley's struggle with himself gives it added interest today. Through the character of Walter Clough, Huxley articulates a more compassionate understanding of the industrial masses in *Now More Than Ever* than he was capable of in the 1920s, and the play helps prepare the ground for his eventual conversion into the more spiritually conscious author of *Eyeless in Gaza* and *Ends and Means* (1937). In this respect, one of the most interesting passages in the play occurs in act III, scene 1. The action takes place in the sparsely furnished parlor of Clough's small house in the north London borough of Camden Town. Walter Clough confesses to Joan Lidgate:

Loving one's neighbour is heroic. Heroic because it's so damnably difficult, the most difficult thing in the world. I've never been able to do it.

JOAN: But if you don't love your neighbour, why do you make sacrifices for him?

CLOUGH: Because I hate injustice, I hate the criminal stupidity and insensitiveness of the people who perpetrate the injustice. But as for saying that I love the men and women I want to save from the exploiters—no; it wouldn't be true. I don't. They bore me. They make me impatient. Why are their minds so limited and personal? Always, me, me, you, you; never an idea or a generalisation. And then that awful complacency and indifference and resignation! The way they put up with intolerable situations! Nobody has a right to be resigned to slums and sweated labour and fat men guzzling at the Savoy. But damn them, they *are* resigned. And then I don't enjoy their pleasures. The movies, and jazz and looking-on at football—it bores me stiff—and, of course what *I* call pleasure they detest. It's a case of chronic and fundamental misunderstanding. Which isn't exactly the best foundation for love. But all the same, I believe it is possible to love one's neighbour even though one may have very little in common with him. I believe there's some way of learning to love him. Through humility, perhaps. *(Pause)*. Queer, the way one finds oneself using religious language. But they knew a lot about human beings, those Christians. If only they hadn't used their knowledge to such bad ends. One's got to take the good and just ruthlessly stamp out the rest. All the disgusting superstitions and the stupid cocksure intolerance. They've got to be fought and conquered and utterly abolished.

Clough's soul-baring foreshadows the direction which Huxley's life and thought were to take from the mid-1930s onward, with a pivotal tilt from ends to means; with a shift in attitude from a superior contempt for the masses to a hesitant affirmation that "it is possible to love one's neighbour even though one may have very little in common with him"; and with the abandonment of an assuredly atheistic position in favor of one where Huxley often found himself "using religious language."

With the reinstatement of *Now More Than Ever* in the Huxley canon, it is now possible to form a complete picture of what is the most fascinating period of his entire career. Though the play was too stationary and talky for its own time, its themes are still relevant to our own, and, directed with flair and pace, the urgency and sense of crisis which prompted Huxley to write the play could still have some impact today.

A Note on the Text

The 92-page revised and corrected typescript of *Now More Than Ever*, which now forms part of the Aldous Huxley Collection at the Harry Ransom Humanities Research Center at the University of Texas at Austin, is the only extant version of the play. In general, the typescript does not contain any deletions or additions of any significance, though Huxley was inclined to lightly rewrite or, more commonly, slightly relocate the odd snatch of dialogue. Our rule has been to take Huxley's revision as an indication of his final preference.

The paper used for pages 7, 52, and 79–80 bears no watermark and the ribbon ink is purple. Pages 84 and 87–90 are watermarked "F. Guermand & Co./ Voiron" and the ribbon ink is purple. Pages 85–86 and 91–92 bear the watermark "Excelsior/ F. Guermand & Co./ Voiron," the ribbon ink once again being purple. Paper with the watermark "L.C.B. Super Papayrus" was used for pages 1, 6, 8–22, 27–37, 43, 45, 48–49, 51, 59–66, 68–72, 74–78, and 81–83; the ink on all these pages is purple. In support of our claim that the HRHRC typescript is the version which Huxley revised and corrected after "several defects" were pointed out to him by Theresa Helburn of the New York Theatre Guild in 1933 (see Introduction), we believe that it is significant that twenty-five leaves of the typescript were produced on a different machine from the typewriter with purple ink which was used to generate the majority of the typescript. On pages 2–5, 23–26, 38–42, 44, 46–47, 50, 53–58, 67, and 73, the paper bears the watermark "Excelsior/ F. Guermand & Co./ Voiron"; the ink on all of these pages is black and the lines are double-spaced. All of these pages contain dialogue by Joan Lidgate, with the exception of pages 46–47, which refer to her, and it seems likely that they represent Huxley's response to Miss Helburn's concern that the only important woman character in the play had not been given enough exposure. Before the play was revised, the curtain was to have been raised at the beginning to reveal the unappetizing Sir Thomas Lupton helping himself to Arthur Lidgate's equally unpalatable sherry before being joined by Lord Upavon ("a quick, active little man, with an intelligent, ugly face. There is something mischievous and gnome-like about him. He has a way of suddenly grinning with malicious mockery") with whom he discusses Lidgate, health, and wealth. Such an opening scene would have signposted Huxley's reason for writing the play much too crudely and far too swiftly. In the revised version, Joan is on the stage alone when the curtain rises at the beginning of act I, and the additional pages emphasize her importance from the outset. Moreover, the sight of her dodging Lupton's clammy-handed attentions just after the play has commenced shows her to be a spirited character with an independent mind. The second major addition (23–26) underscores Joan's growing disaffection with her privileged milieu, and the third (38–42) reinforces her quest for a more meaningful *modus vivendi*. It appears that Huxley intercalated his new leaves at the appropriate points of his typescript and then lightly revised the whole script in pen. The dialogue on sixty-seven pages is single-spaced and is characterized by an irregular lowercase *w* caused by a stiff key on Huxley's typewriter. The dialogue on the twenty-five additional pages, on the other hand, is consistently double-spaced and betrays no sign of the idiosyncratic *w*. Huxley's use of a second typewriter is explained by the fact that he left his usual one behind in New York before embarking on a sea journey to Central America in 1933. In a letter of 24 May 1933 he thanks Eugene Saxton, his New York publisher, for finding it and arranging to have it sent to London.[60]

We have silently capitalized certain terms of address or titles (such as "daddy" and "countess") and we have de-hyphenated words such as "to-day" and "good-bye" in accordance with modern usage. Huxley's predominantly British English orthography has been retained; the occasional preference for *z* rather than *s* in *-ize* is authorial, not editorial. A small number of typographical errors have been corrected, and a few other inconsistencies (for example, Upavon is incorrectly addressed as "Tom," rather than "Jack" on two occasions in the typescript) have been ironed out.

Act I

The library at Monmouth House, Berkeley Square, London.

Act II

SCENE 1. Hyde Park, London, three weeks later.
SCENE 2. The library at Monmouth House, six weeks later.

Act III

SCENE 1. Walter Clough's living room, Camden Town, London, one month later.
SCENE 2. The library at Monmouth House, same evening.

Epilogue

The library at Monmouth House, four days later.

Act I

The library at Monmouth House, Berkeley Square.[1] *A noble, late Georgian room, lined with bookshelves. There are busts on pedestals. On the left a marble fireplace surmounted by the full-length portrait of an eighteenth-century Duke of Monmouth. Two windows in the back wall, set in deep embrasures, with shelves between them; a door on the right, a large writing table in the centre of the room. All the furniture is in eighteenth-century mahogany. It is an evening in winter. The curtains are drawn, the lights are turned on. A fire burns in the grate. On a small table near the fireplace stands a tray with bottles and glasses.* JOAN *is alone in the room when the curtain rises. She sits, reading, in one of the window embrasures, where she cannot be seen from the door. Enter* FOOTMAN, *followed by* SIR THOMAS LUPTON*[2].* LUPTON *is a gross, red-faced, greasily prosperous-looking man in the fifties.*

FOOTMAN: Mr. Lidgate will be down in a moment, sir. I'll go and tell him you're here.

*(*LUPTON *crosses the room and, standing in front of the fire, begins meditatively to pick his teeth, interrupting the process only to belch.* JOAN *meanwhile puts her book down on the seat beside her and rising tries to tiptoe away unheard and unseen towards the door. A sound causes* LUPTON *to turn round.* JOAN *says "Damn!" under her breath, then resigns herself to being caught.)*

LUPTON: Why, Joan, my dear child! Where were you hiding? *(He hurries across the room towards her, putting away his toothpick as he goes.)* This is a pleasure, Joan. *(He shakes her hand and continues to hold it, interminably.)* By the way, I suppose I still may call you Joan—in spite of your being so grown-up. May I?

JOAN: You can call me Jehoshaphat,[3] if it gives you any pleasure.

LUPTON: *(Goggling sentimentally.)* When I think that you were a little girl with a pig tail, when first I saw you. *(He is still holding her right*

5

hand in his and now, with his left, he pats it. JOAN *meanwhile is visibly trying to break loose.)* It seems only yesterday. And now . . . now you're a woman, Joan. A beautiful woman. It's extraordinary. *(He sighs.)*

JOAN: *(Freeing herself at last and walking towards the fireplace.)* Extraordinary? But what did you expect me to grow into? A beautiful chimpanzee?⁴ *(Looking at her watch.)* Oh, it's late. I must go and dress. Goodbye, Sir Thomas.

LUPTON: Why don't you call me Uncle Tom, as you used to?

JOAN: *(Shrugging her shoulders.)* All right, then. A rose by any other name would smell as sweet, Uncle Tom. *(Laughing.)* I shall think of you in your cabin—Uncle Tom's Cabin in Upper Brook Street.⁵ With all the piccaninnies. And the black mammy. *(Her laughter becomes uncontrollable.)* Oh dear, oh dear. It's a lovely thought. Good night, Uncle Tom.

LUPTON: Won't you keep me company for a moment?

JOAN: Sorry. We're going to the theatre. Dinner's early. I've got to go and get dressed. *(She walks towards the door.* LUPTON *follows and lays a hand on her arm.)*

LUPTON: One evening you must come out with me, Joan. We'll have a nice little dinner first . . .

JOAN: At the cabin?

LUPTON: And then we'll go to a show.

JOAN: With black mammy as a chaperon. I insist on that.

LUPTON: Now do be serious, Joan. *(Sentimentally.)* It would be such fun, wouldn't it? *(He waits for her to reply; but she says nothing.)* What about next Tuesday?

JOAN: *(Moving again towards the door.)* Tuesday I'm engaged.

LUPTON: Wednesday, then.

JOAN: No, that's no good either.

LUPTON: Well, Thursday.

JOAN: Now look here, Sir Thomas—I mean Uncle Tom—I really can't settle it now. I shall have to look in my engagement book. Besides,

LUPTON: Yes; first catch your amalgamation, then cook it.[11] How near are you to catching, Arthur?

LIDGATE: Pretty close. Closer than anyone thinks. They've got to come in, whether they want to or not. Circumstances are on my side. It's their only way of reducing production costs.

LUPTON: The only way? What about wages? Wages have got to come down, I tell you. They've got to come down. If only we had a government with a bit of courage and . . . and vision . . . .

LIDGATE: Yes, yes. But let's stick to facts. Given the facts, amalgamation is their only method of reducing costs. They're being pushed towards it, as I pull. The worst trouble is with the older men. I offer them an alternative to bankruptcy. But you'd really think they preferred bankruptcy. Anything rather than change their habits and resign their powers. Going down with the ship is all very well, as I was saying to old Wagstaffe only today. (You know, Wagstaffe from Middlesbrough.[12]) Very well indeed, I said. But keeping the ship afloat is still better. But he doesn't want the ship to float unless he's the captain. He just refuses to understand.

UPAVON: Probably he can't understand, poor old devil. How much do you suppose *you'll* understand when you're a tottering old fossil of eighty?

LUPTON: *(Who is helping himself to more drink.)* I don't see why one should necessarily become a fossil when one's old.

UPAVON: No, I agree; you'll get out of the difficulty by becoming a corpse first.

LUPTON: What?

UPAVON: Diabetes and high blood pressure.

LUPTON: High? What do you know about it? It's not in the least high. *(But he puts down the bottle without filling his glass.)* Not in the least. *(Looking at his watch.)* Six-twenty-five. I must be off.

LIDGATE: Must you? *(He rings the bell by the fireplace.)* I'm sorry.

LUPTON: If there are any new developments, you'll keep me posted, won't you?

LIDGATE: Of course.

LUPTON: Well, goodbye, Arthur. So long, Upavon.

UPAVON: *(Waves his hand, grinning, as he does so, with mischievous irony.* LUPTON *goes out.)* You know, Arthur, you have some awful friends.

LIDGATE: *(Apologetically.)* He has the most astonishing nose for speculation. I've never known anyone like him. Besides, he's Wertheim's representative here.

UPAVON: I know, I know. But that doesn't make him more appetizing, does it?

LIDGATE: Poor old Lupton!

UPAVON: Poor old Arthur, on the contrary. The trouble with business associates is that they *will* insist on being treated as friends. If you won't pretend to be friendly, they're annoyed and refuse to do any more business.

LIDGATE: Lupton's not such a bad chap, really.

UPAVON: Yes, he is. But, unfortunately, he's useful. And now let's disinfect the mental atmosphere and talk about something else. How's your battle with the issuing houses going?

LIDGATE: It's over; I've won. They wouldn't reduce their commission, and I've undercut them. I'm issuing three big municipal loans this winter. Portsmouth, Coventry, Nottingham.[13] Over five millions in all. It won't mean a great return in cash, with the commission down to where I've brought it. But it'll mean a lot of fresh credit—the chance to launch out somewhere new.

UPAVON: *(Laughing.)* That's the spirit, Arthur! What's it to be this time?

LIDGATE: Well, there's cotton. I've been nosing around a bit. Gosh, the chaos! You've no conception. But I've made some friends up there in Lancashire. And I've got the rough outlines of a plan.[14] I'll explain it to you, Jack. The thing is to begin on the selling organizations. Once we've got those under control, we can . . .

(Enter FOOTMAN *with a card on a salver.)*

What is it?

FOOTMAN: A gentleman has called to see you, sir. He says he has an appointment.

LIDGATE: *(Looking at the card.)* Yes, of course. I'd forgotten. Show him in. *(Exit* FOOTMAN.*)* Do you mind, Jack? I've made the man come up specially from the country. You understand?

UPAVON: Of course. I'll clear out. *(He makes as if to rise; but* LID-GATE *pushes him back into his seat.)*

LIDGATE: No, no, don't go. I'll tell you who the fellow is. He's a sort of writer. Not that I've ever read anything he wrote. But they say he's quite good in his line. I met him at Lady Hinksey's. He's an amusing fellow. Interesting too. I'd an idea of taking him on as a sort of secretary.

UPAVON: Another secretary?

LIDGATE: A different kind of secretary. You see I . . . but here he is. *(The door opens. The* FOOTMAN *announces "Mr. Barmby."*[15] *Enter* PHILIP BARMBY.*)* So glad you were able to come, Mr. Barmby. Do you know my old friend, Lord Upavon?

BARMBY: Only from the caricatures. *(Shakes hands with* UPAVON.*)*

LIDGATE: Sherry, Mr. Barmby? Or vermouth? Or gin?

BARMBY: Vermouth, please. *(He looks round him.)* My word, this is a magnificent room! *(Glancing at the portrait over the mantelpiece.)* Romney, alas! Why did he have to go and choose the worst painter of the period? Thank you. *(Taking the glass from* LIDGATE.*)* I say, these books! What a superb set of Voltaire! *(He puts down his glass and pulls out a volume.)* Oh, it's the Kehl edition of 1785—the one Voltaire himself worked on. Lovely! *(Puts it back and takes up his glass again.)* I must say, I envy you this library, Mr. Lidgate.

LIDGATE: I'm ashamed to say I've never yet taken a book out of the shelves. I don't ever seem to have the time. And even if I had, I shouldn't know where to begin. You'd know, because you're an educated man. I'm not. I never had a proper education.

BARMBY: No proper education in my line, if you like. But then I'm equally uneducated in yours. I mean, if you were to ask me what the difference was between a Bill of Exchange and a Bill of Lading, I simply shouldn't be able to answer.

LIDGATE: And nobody would think any the worse of you for that. But they *would* think the worse of me, if I said I'd never read a word of your Voltaire there. *(Pointing towards the bookshelf.)*

BARMBY: Yes, I admit my kind of education has more prestige than yours. It has more even than scientific education. Here I am—just a dilettante with a gift of the gab; and yet I cut much more ice than any scientific man short of a first-class genius. Most convenient for me, of course. But it's intrinsically rather absurd. Well, *(he raises his glass)* long may the absurdity persist! *(He drinks.)*

UPAVON: It'll persist as long as ignorance and stupidity persist. Take my job, Mr. Barmby—newspapers. Who are the people I pay the big prices to? Not to the men who actually discover things, but to the ones who know how to make the public understand—or at any rate, make them *think* they understand—what it's all about. Just consider the economics of scientific discovery. The first account of it is published in some technical journal. Needless to say, the contribution isn't paid for. Then comes somebody like you, somebody with a general education and a gift of the gab; he reads the original communication, makes a re-hash of it for popular consumption, sends it to one of my papers and promptly receives a cheque for twenty guineas. But that's only the beginning. If he has any sense, he'll write another article for one of the high-brow weeklies—six guineas—another for syndication in America—thirty or forty—a broadcast talk—twenty-five—and a lecture, which he can go on repeating indefinitely at anything from five to fifteen or twenty guineas an evening. By the time he's finished, he may have made a small fortune out of a discovery, for which the original discoverer has received exactly nought pounds, zero shillings and no pence.

(Enter MR. SPENCE *a grey little man of around sixty. He walks on tiptoe. His manner is deprecating. He holds up a batch of letters and faintly whispers, "Letters to sign, sir" to* LIDGATE, *who beckons him to the table, where he sits down, reading and signing throughout the succeeding scene.)*

BARMBY: Well, in the first place, I don't know in detail what your plan is; and, in the second, I haven't got time to launch out into a discourse on economics. But surely it must be sufficiently obvious by this time that any plan based on the private ownership of industry is quite hopeless.[19]

LIDGATE: May I ask why?

BARMBY: Well, for all the obvious reasons. For you private owners, wages are a cost. You've got to keep them down. You're forced to introduce machines to displace wage-earners. In other words, you're forced to reduce the number of people who can consume your products. Under the profit-making system, you can never distribute enough purchasing power to absorb your production. So you've got to have exports.

SPENCE: Exports! Exactly! That's what we're working for—to capture the export trade.

BARMBY: Of course, you are. And what do you do when you've captured it? You take imports in exchange. But you can never take enough imports to balance your exports. Why not? For the good reason that consumers who haven't got enough purchasing power to buy what you produce at home are equally incapable of buying the equivalent of your production in imports. What do you do about it? You have no alternative. The only way you can take payment for your exports is in capital investments abroad. For example, you export a certain number of million pounds' worth of iron and steel; you take imports for as much as, under your idiotic financial system, the home consumer can afford to buy; and the remainder you invest in the country to which you've exported your stuff.

SPENCE: And very sensible, if the investment's sound.

BARMBY: Wait a minute, Mr. Spence! What does it mean exactly when your investment is sound? It simply means this: that these new industries that you've financed, are so efficient that they can sell large quantities of their products.

SPENCE: Exactly.

BARMBY: But the more they sell, the less you sell. You've raised up a competitor against yourselves. There's a struggle, which ends, invariably, in the same way: the government of the country in which you've invested your profits sticks up a tariff against you. You're shut out of yet another market. And not only that: you've got a new competitor for such markets as remain. And, of course, they don't remain very long. There are fewer and fewer of them every year. Because, inevitably, you go on doing exactly the same thing—investing what you won't allow your home-consumers to take as imports in new production abroad. Financing more and more rivals; driving more and more governments to set up protective tariffs against you.

SPENCE: *(Breaking out again.)* But if you reduce costs enough, tariffs don't matter. Nor does competition. It's all a question of reducing costs. And that's just what we're doing; aren't we, sir? *(To* LIDGATE. *Then, turning again to* BARMBY.*)* I don't think you realize what we've done already. I could give you figures about electrical equipment, and coal, and artificial resins—you'd be astonished. And then the savings we're planning for iron and steel. I tell you, you don't realize.

BARMBY: On the contrary, Mr. Spence, I know how conscientiously you're trying to reduce the purchasing power of the home consumer so as to compete with your rivals abroad. It's admirable! And what huge sums you're investing overseas, in spite of the slump! Millions and millions to finance still more competitors! And when you've put them on their feet, you'll have to reduce home purchasing power still further in order to be able to compete with them. And after you've finally discharged all the wage earners that can be discharged, after you've reduced the wages of the rest to a point at which they can't consume anything but bread and water, then, when you're at last in a position to cut out your rivals and get through the tariff barriers, what follows?

SPENCE: *(Triumphantly.)* Why! you capture the trade!

BARMBY: No you don't; what follows is that the rest of the world starts talking about "unfair competition" and "dumping" and proceeds to close its frontiers. You won't be allowed to export a halfpennyworth of anything anywhere. After which there'll be nothing to do but declare war. May I take a drop more vermouth?

LIDGATE: *(Still reading and signing.)* Do.

SPENCE: *(Very much agitated.)* You make it sound all very plausible, I know. But you're wrong somewhere. I feel it in my bones that you're wrong.

BARMBY: You're like all the politicians and businessmen I've ever talked to, Mr. Spence. They always feel things in their bones. Never by any chance in their heads.

LIDGATE: *(Putting down his pen.)* There! Now I'm ready to come to the rescue. *(He pats* SPENCE'S *arm.* SPENCE *smiles at him with a dog-like devotion.)* You've been mangling my poor lieutenant in the most bloodthirsty way, Mr. Barmby.

SPENCE: He's wrong. I'm convinced he's wrong.

LIDGATE: Right in theory, perhaps. But wrong in practice.

BARMBY: Practice? Heaven preserve me from practice! I've never done any practice in my life.

LIDGATE: Which is why you're in the wrong. Because when you practice, you're always feeling your way towards compromises and working arrangements. Theoretically, capitalism may not work under a system of power production. But in practice, somehow or other, we make it work.

BARMBY: Do you? I confess I hadn't noticed it.

LIDGATE: Well, the proof is that you've still got an income.

BARMBY: Once more, alas, I hadn't noticed it.

LIDGATE: According to the rules of logic, we've doubtless got no right to exist. But all the same, we do exist. *(He looks at his watch.)* Nearly a quarter to, Spence. Time to ring up the American office. Go and get me New York, will you?

SPENCE: Very well, sir. *(He picks up the letters and prepares to go.)*

LIDGATE: Thank you so much. *(Exit* SPENCE.*)* It's a great boon, this trans-Atlantic telephone.[20] You've no idea how it simplifies matters if one's operating on the stock market.

BARMBY: Does it?

LIDGATE: It makes all the difference.

BARMBY: Faraday and Clerk Maxwell[21] haven't lived in vain.

LIDGATE: It's no good making that kind of joke to an uneducated man, Mr. Barmby. Who was Clerk Maxwell? I've never heard of him.

BARMBY: Well, yes, I admit, that does slightly blunt the point of the remark.

LIDGATE: There's a terrible list of things and names I've never heard of. And, as a matter of fact, Mr. Barmby, it's about that I asked you to come up and see me. I had an idea—perhaps it's a hopelessly stupid idea—I give you leave to laugh at me if you think so—I had an idea that perhaps you might be persuaded to come and be—well, I don't know how to describe it exactly—a kind of resident philosopher here in Monmouth House—a kind of secretary for culture, if you see what I mean.

BARMBY: I confess I don't, exactly.

LIDGATE: I'll explain to you what I want. I want to live in this house as though—well, as though I belonged to it—as though I weren't what in fact I am: just a rich upstart, without education, without culture, without traditions. You may ask why I went and shoved myself into a place where I obviously don't belong. Partly for publicity's sake: it's a good advertisement. Partly vanity, no doubt. And then the pleasures of taking a kind of revenge on all these umpteenth dukes. *(Waving his hand towards the portrait over the mantelpiece.)* Me, the son of a Brondesbury ironmonger, sitting in Monmouth House, while His Grace cools his heels outside. It's childish, no doubt; but the thought gives me a certain satisfaction.[22]

BARMBY: I know it would give me an enormous pleasure.

LIDGATE: And then there's another reason—the chief reason—and that's my daughter. You've never met Joan, have you? *(BARMBY shakes his head.)* Well, she's an only child. Her mother died when she was quite a baby. I've spoilt her, of course. I dare say I'm a bit weak-minded about her. But, after all, what a blessing it is to have something one can be weak-minded about! Anyhow, there she is, just coming out into the world. I wanted her to make her entrance in the best possible style. Monmouth House was to let. So here I am.

BARMBY: Of course. Most comprehensible.

LIDGATE: Good. You understand why I'm here. And now can you also understand that, being here, I don't want to seem too grotesquely out of the picture?

BARMBY: Perfectly.

LIDGATE: For Joan's sake even more than for my own. Well, my idea was this: to persuade you to come and help me adjust myself to these surroundings.

BARMBY: How?

LIDGATE: We shall have to find out by experiment. Meanwhile I can only make a few suggestions. Take art, for example. Why is that picture a good one, or a bad one, whichever the case may be? What's the difference between Chippendale and Jacobean?²³ Who was Michelangelo? How do I tell, without looking at the name underneath, which of those busts is a Roman Emperor and which is an umpteenth duke? You could begin by teaching me to answer those questions. At present I have to be dumb when educated people are talking—hold my tongue for fear of saying something ludicrous. I want you to give me a little coaching, so that I needn't be afraid.

BARMBY: Well, I've no doubt something might be done.

LIDGATE: That's one side of the business: making me fit for civilized society. Another side, no less important, would be persuading the civilized society to come to me.

BARMBY: What?

LIDGATE: I find it so horribly difficult to get into touch with any intelligent, interesting people. Titles, yes; and the sort of people you see pictures of in the *Sketch*²⁴—they're easy enough to get hold of. Too easy. They seem to come in swarms. But, my God, they're boring! Worse even than City men. And uneducated! I want to meet people who've got an idea in their heads. And I want Joan to meet them. She's worth more than these imbecile young creatures she sees now.

BARMBY: That must be the one great disadvantage of being rich—having to associate with the other rich.

LIDGATE: Exactly. Well, I don't want to associate with the other rich.

BARMBY: You can't help it. Deep calls to deep.[25] There's no escape.

LIDGATE: But at least I can take an occasional holiday. And that's what I want you to arrange for me. Invite your friends to the house here. Could you do that?

BARMBY: Give them food and drink, and there'll be no holding them back.

LIDGATE: You don't take a very high view of your fellow men, do you, Mr. Barmby?

BARMBY: The low view is safer. You don't have so far to fall, if they let you down. And if ever they let you up, what an unexpected pleasure! Well, as I was saying, they'll come all right, if you ask them.

LIDGATE: And would you be prepared to carry the invitations?

BARMBY: Well . . . *(He hesitates.)*

LIDGATE: But of course, there's no reason why you should decide at once.

BARMBY: I'll be frank with you. The job tempts me. It's comfortable, it's easy. No work to speak of; and I do so detest every form of work! And then this library—it makes one's mouth water. The only disadvantage . . . *(He hesitates.)*

LIDGATE: Is what?

BARMBY: Well, that I shall be a parasite, a kind of court jester.

LIDGATE: No, no. The resident philosopher.

BARMBY: It comes to the same thing. Philosophers who reside at courts automatically become jesters.

LIDGATE: I assure you . . .

BARMBY: *(Shrugging his shoulders.)* But, after all, what does it matter? Why shouldn't one be a parasite? *(Turning to* LIDGATE.*)* What had you thought of as a wage, Mr. Lidgate?

LIDGATE: *(Embarrassed.)* Oh, I don't know. Say, fifty pounds a month.

BARMBY: Done! When do you want me to come?

LIDGATE: Whenever you like. The sooner the better.

BARMBY: All right, then. The day after tomorrow.

LIDGATE: Excellent. And now please don't let me hear any more talk about parasites. I don't want you to feel that you've sacrificed the smallest particle of your independence. If you did feel that, I tell you frankly that you'd lose a great part of your value for me. I like these savage criticisms of yours. They are stimulating; they keep my mind awake. You mustn't think you've got to stop criticizing, just because I'm paying you a salary. On the contrary.

BARMBY: Don't worry Mr. Lidgate. Being rude is one of the main functions of the court fool. I promise you I'll . . .

(Enter JOAN LIDGATE; *she has changed into an evening frock.)*

JOAN: Oh, I'm sorry, Daddy, I thought you were alone.

LIDGATE: Come in, come in. This is Mr. Barmby, Joan. *(*BARMBY *and* JOAN *shake hands.)* Mr. Barmby has consented to come and be my secretary.

JOAN: What? Instead of Mr. Spence? You've not sent away poor old Mr. Spence!

LIDGATE: No, no. Of course not.

BARMBY: Mr. Spence still remains the grand vizier. I've been taken on as the court fool.

JOAN: You're not the Barmby who writes things in the *Week-End Review*,[26] by any chance?

BARMBY: Alas, I am.

JOAN: There's no alas about it. I think some of them are most frightfully good—your articles, I mean. Have you ever written a book?

BARMBY: Never.

JOAN: You ought to.

BARMBY: I know I ought to.

JOAN: Then why don't you?

BARMBY: Laziness, that's all.

JOAN: I don't think that's any excuse. My goodness, I wouldn't be lazy, if there were something I could do well. But there isn't. How I envy people like you and Daddy—people who know what they ought to do because they've got some talent that drives them on! People like me are in the hands of chance. There's no reason why they should do one thing rather than another. If they do finally end by tumbling into some groove, it's just because they happen to get married, or have to make a living. I think it's humiliating.

LIDGATE: *(Putting his arms round her, affectionately.)* How disgustingly insipid life would be, if there weren't something to grumble at!

JOAN: *(Indignantly.)* I'm not grumbling. I'm just stating facts.

BARMBY: But that's the definition of grumbling.

LIDGATE: Tell me, who are we going out with tonight?

JOAN: Only Peggy and Ted Monmouth.

LIDGATE: What, His Grace?

JOAN: But he's quite harmless, Daddy.

LIDGATE: That's just what he isn't. He'll go and stick us in his horrible gossip column tomorrow.

JOAN: I've made him promise he wouldn't.

LIDGATE: Gossip-writing dukes![27] I do think it's a bit thick, don't you Mr. Barmby?

BARMBY: Well, I confess, it's not exactly my idea of *noblesse oblige*.

JOAN: But the poor lamb's got to make his living.

LIDGATE: Well, let him choose another profession.

JOAN: But which? He's never been educated, he's got no talents. What else can he do except write gossip? And if the people who read Uppy's papers want that sort of drivel, why shouldn't he give it them?

BARMBY: Unanswerable, Miss Lidgate! *(Getting up from his chair.)*

But I must be going, I'm afraid. Goodbye. *(Shakes hands, then turns to* LIDGATE.*)* Goodbye.

LIDGATE: Then I can expect you the day after tomorrow.

BARMBY: Without fail.

LIDGATE: Excellent. *(*BARMBY *goes out.)* What do you think of him, Joan?

JOAN: Somehow he makes me rather sad.

LIDGATE: Sad?

JOAN: He's so . . . I don't know . . . so resigned. The way he laughs at everything including himself.[28] People oughtn't to do that. They ought to look ferocious, and put down their heads, and charge, like a bull. *(She makes as if to charge into the middle of her father's waistcoat.)*

LIDGATE: *(Keeping her off.)* Here! Hi! I'm not a toreador.

JOAN: *(Straightening herself up, and still laughing.)* But you are. You are. And that's just why I adore you. *(She throws her arms round his neck and kisses him.)* The most ferocious old matador. *(In another tone.)* Seriously, you know, I could never marry a man who wasn't a bit of a bull fighter.

LIDGATE: Well, I hope that rules out His Grace.

JOAN: What, Ted? Do you mean to say that you'd imagined . . .

LIDGATE: *(Rather embarrassed.)* Well, I'd noticed him buzzing round a good deal recently.

JOAN: But did you think I was listening to the buzz?

LIDGATE: *(Shrugging his shoulders uncomfortably.)* One never knows.

JOAN: Well, all I can say is that you ought to know. Ted, indeed! My good man! You must have an Oedipus complex to imagine such things. Jealous of poor little Ted!

LIDGATE: *(Shocked.)* Joan! How can you talk like that?

JOAN: Seriously, Daddy, I couldn't stand a man who was content to sit and do nothing. People who do nothing—you know, they're terrible really—even when they're nice people. Peggy and Diana and Ted and Sibyl and all the rest of them. I like them a lot, you know. But all the same they're terrible. And I'm so frightened of becoming like them. And if I did, you know it would be a bit your fault, Daddy.

LIDGATE: *My* fault? Why?

JOAN: For bringing me up in such a ridiculous way.

LIDGATE: But, my darling, you had the best education I knew how to give you.

JOAN: I know. That's just what I complain of. Years and years of the most expensive schools; and at the end of it all, there's nothing I know how to do. Absolutely nothing. You'd have done better to pitchfork me into the world at sixteen—the same as was done to you. Then I should have damn well had to learn something—if only to darn my own stockings. As it is . . . *(She shrugs her shoulders despairingly.)*

LIDGATE: But, Joan, you speak as though everything were over and finished. It isn't. You're still at the beginning. You can study what you like, wherever you like. Surely you know that. I'm ready to do anything you want—anything that will make you happy.

JOAN: Oh, I know you are, Daddy. And I'm grateful. Only somehow it only makes things worse. When there are such a lot of alternatives, one ends by choosing none of them. One just drifts along, doing nothing.

LIDGATE: Doesn't that mean you're happier doing nothing?

JOAN: No, of course it doesn't.

LIDGATE: But then why . . .

JOAN: It's all this damned freedom you've given me. Freedom's terrible you know. Freedom's a burden. The burden of being able to do whatever one wants. I sometimes think it would be nice to be a nun. Only of course I couldn't stand all that going to church. Oh dear! *(She sighs.)* Let's change the subject. I don't see why I should make you miserable with my silly complaining. *(She sits on his knee.)* How was the bull-fighting today?

LIDGATE: Oh, not so bad.

JOAN: I hope you punctured a lot of those greasy old oxen from Lombard Street.²⁹ Lousy brutes! My word, how I should like to stick a banderillo into old Lupton, for example! *(She makes the gesture of jabbing home the dart, accompanying the movement with an expressive click of the tongue.)* Do you know that he actually tried to hold my hand this evening?

LIDGATE: *(Indignantly.)* You don't mean to say he dared to . . .

JOAN: Oh, it was all very pure and uncle-ish. But he's one of those people whose hands are always *wet.* Ugh! *(She makes a grimace and shudders.)* Too revolting! Next time he wants to do that uncle business, I shall ask him to put on gloves.

LIDGATE: *(Still angry.)* It's outrageous. I shall tell him he's got to behave himself.

JOAN: Now, don't start being Oedipus-ish again. You'll make yourself ridiculous. Leave me to deal with my own uncles. I'm perfectly capable of looking after myself. Don't you believe it?

LIDGATE: Yes, I suppose you are. But all the same . . .

(Enter FOOTMAN, *who announces, "His Grace the Duke of Monmouth."* THE DUKE *is a rather silly looking, but elaborately affected, young man in the early twenties.)*

JOAN: *(Going to meet him.)* Hullo, Ted.

MONMOUTH: Joan darling!

JOAN: Welcome to the home of your ancestors. I wonder what *they* think of you, by the way. *(She lays her hands on his shoulders and, at arm's length, looks intently into his face; then shakes her head.)* Poor ancestors! I'm glad I haven't got any. *(She turns away, and* MONMOUTH *goes and shakes hands with* LIDGATE.)

LIDGATE: Good evening, Ted.

JOAN: Needless to say, Peggy's going to be late.

MONMOUTH: She does it on purpose.

LIDGATE: What on earth for?

MONMOUTH: To make people take notice of her. When you've got no other way of attracting attention, unpunctuality will always do the trick.

JOAN: Well, of all the catty remarks! *(Enter* SPENCE.*)* Hullo, Mr. Spence. I haven't seen you for days. How are you?

SPENCE: Very well, thanks, Miss Joan. And I was to give you kindest regards from my sister. She *did* enjoy your visit, Miss Joan. She really did. *(To* LIDGATE.*)* Your call's just coming through, Mr. Lidgate.

LIDGATE: The New York call? *(*SPENCE *nods. He gets up and turns to* JOAN.*)* I shall be five minutes at least. If Peggy comes before I'm through, start dinner without me.

JOAN: Anyhow *you'll* stay with us, Mr. Spence, and tell us about your sister.

LIDGATE: No, I'm afraid I need him. There'll be things to take down.

SPENCE: I'm sorry, Miss Joan. *(They go out.)*

MONMOUTH: Why were you so anxious for that old fool to stay, Joan?

JOAN: He's not an old fool. And I'm very fond of him. And he looks after his invalid sister—which is more than you'd ever do, if you had an invalid sister, Ted.

MONMOUTH: Oh, damn his sister! You asked him to stay because you didn't want to be alone with me.

JOAN: No, I didn't.

MONMOUTH: Yes, you did.

JOAN: I didn't.

MONMOUTH: I tell you, you did.

JOAN: All right then I did. And please, now, don't start proving I was right in not wanting to be alone with you.

MONMOUTH: *(In a languishing tone.)* Listen, Joan. *(She averts her head.)* Joan, I beg you . . .

JOAN: Must we go through all this again?

MONMOUTH: But, Joan, I love you.

JOAN: No, you don't. Not more than you love Peggy, or Diana, or Sybil.

MONMOUTH: Darling, I swear . . .

JOAN: And much less than you love that little tart who's dancing at the Hippodrome.[30]

MONMOUTH: *(Startled and indignant.)* Really, Joan . . .

JOAN: Well, isn't she a tart?

MONMOUTH: *(Who has recovered his presence of mind loftily.)* To start with I really don't know who you're referring to.

JOAN: O-O-OH! *(She puts her hand over her mouth.)* That's a good one, Ted!

MONMOUTH: I assure you . . .

JOAN: Ted, I think it would be safer if we changed the subject.

MONMOUTH: *(With dignity.)* Just as you like, Joan.

JOAN: Oh, not for my sake. I'm quite ready to go on talking about your little friend at the Hippodrome. I only thought that perhaps you weren't quite so keen.

MONMOUTH: *(Sounding the pathetic note once more.)* Why are you always so cruel, Joan? Making a joke of my deepest feelings . . .

JOAN: Hippodrome, Hippodrome! *(MONMOUTH covers his face with his hands.)* Now look here, Ted, don't be an ass. Why must you go and spoil everything? It was all such fun, before you started this stupid business. Why shouldn't we go on having fun? If only you'd behave like a reasonable creature! I don't want to quarrel with you. I hate quarreling. I want to be friends with you.

MONMOUTH: *(Looking up at last, and in a resigned voice.)* All right then, Joan, let's be friends . . .

JOAN: But not in that tone, man. That's not being friendly; that's being more in sorrow than in anger. Cheerful! *(She gives him a terrific slap on the back that makes him gasp.)* More spirit! *(Yet another smack.)* More guts! *(Another.)*

MONMOUTH: Here, steady on, Joan!

JOAN: Guts! *(She gives him a still more violent slap. The door opens and the* FOOTMAN *announces, "Miss Endicott." Enter* PEGGY ENDICOTT. JOAN *flies to meet her.)* At last, Peggy darling! At last! I thought you were never coming.

PEGGY: Sweet, I'm *so* sorry. But if you knew what complications! In *Chel*sea,[31] of all places. Ted, darling, you look more *rad*iant than ever.

MONMOUTH: Radiant? Of all the damn insults!

PEGGY: Such a Dostoe*vsk*yan cocktail party at the Johnstones'. I can't des*cribe* to you the state poor Madge was in. Because, you see, Tony Lamond was there—Tony of all people! *And* Patricia! Yes, my dear. *And* Patricia.

(Enter BUTLER.*)*

BUTLER: Dinner is served.

JOAN: *(Moving towards the door.)* And what happened?

PEGGY: What *happened?* Well, really, can I *poss*ibly tell you in front of Ted?

MONMOUTH: Please, please, you know how discreet I am.

PEGGY: Oh, it's not *that* I'm bothering about. It's my maiden blushes. Well, I'll tell you . . . *(They pass through the door, and the* CUR-TAIN *which has been slowly descending finally blots them out.)*

Act II

Scene 1

Hyde Park on a Sunday afternoon[32] *three weeks later. The distances are grey and filmy with mist. The bare trees are faintly seen across the expanses of grass. In the foreground a wide gravelled path. Half way up the stage, from right and left, project two promontories of evergreen shrubbery, fenced off from the gravel, leaving at the centre a wide opening, through which one sees the misty distance. This opening gives access to another path running parallel to the first behind the shrubberies.*

Front, left, stands a small portable harmonium, which is being played, as the curtain rises, by a melancholy looking man, while four devoted females stand round singing a hymn.

Perched on a soap box in the middle of the stage stands a harmless LUNATIC *with long, flowing hair, who smiles to himself, radiantly happy, while he pours out the interminable history of his martyrdoms. He has a way, while he speaks, of shutting his eyes as though he were contemplating some inward vision; then briefly opening them to look at his audience.*

Behind the shrubbery on the right we see WALTER CLOUGH.[33] *He is standing on a fairly high platform, so that he is visible from the waist up. On the extreme right, also behind the shrubbery, are visible the heads of the people standing in the front line of the crowd that is listening to him. One must imagine the rest of the crowd extending far back into the wings.* CLOUGH *is talking straight out of the stage towards the right, presenting his right profile to the audience. Above his head, a board on a pole bears the emblem of the hammer and sickle and the words "Communist Party of Great Britain." On the side of the shrubbery nearer to the audience stands a row of green iron chairs. Throughout the scene people are continually strolling up and down the two paths on either side of the shrubberies, forming groups round the* HYMN SINGERS *or the* LUNATIC *or* CLOUGH, *then drifting on again. The singing is heard before the curtain rises and as it goes up, we find the harmonium in full blast, the four females warbling open-mouthed. There are only two or three people listening to them.*

SINGERS: Art thou weary, art thou languid,
              Art thou sore distrest?
              "Come to me," saith One, "and coming
              Be at rest!"[34]

(They go on singing faintly, so that one can hear what the others are saying.)

CLOUGH: ... to the oppressed millions of the working classes—it's to them we make our appeal. Oppressed millions, I repeat. But it seems a contradiction in terms. Millions are stronger than a few. Then why are the millions oppressed by the few? Because they let themselves be oppressed. Because they haven't got the guts to turn against their oppressors. Where there's a will, there's a way. What you English working men need is will, will, will! *(Applause from the crowd.)* Yes, you applaud. But when you've done applauding you slouch home and you do nothing—Nothing! Now, listen here. *(He speaks in a lower voice, more argumentatively, leaning down towards his hearers, so that we no longer hear what he says.)*

LUNATIC: And then, my friends, *(three jeering hobbledehoys are all his audience)* to the eternal disgrace of British Justice—to its eternal disgrace, I tell you, my enemies were allowed to accomplish their fell designs upon me. I was dragged away—yes, ladies and gentlemen, dragged away from hearth and home—and flung into a noisome dungeon, in the common asylum.

BOY: Garn, they ought to have kept you there.

LUNATIC: Yes, ladies and gentlemen, the common asylum, the ... *(The boys take up his refrain and repeat with him in unison, "the common asylum.")*

LUNATIC: But justice must prevail in the long run, ladies and gentlemen. Justice must inevitably prevail.

BOY: Oh, shut it! *(They move away.)*

LUNATIC: All I want ... *(Opens his eyes and looks around; perceiving that he has no audience, he stops speaking, but continues to smile to himself, to make strange gestures; his lips move. The* HYMN SINGERS *raise their voices a little and we hear:)*

people who think they've got something better to do. We've got no use for fine-weather enthusiasts,—the ones who slink away the moment things go badly. We've got no use for playboys and sensation-mongers: revolution isn't a sport or a thrill-factory. It's a religion, it's a man's whole life, it's the reason why he exists—and if it isn't these things, then it's nothing, it's not worth making, not worth asking recruits for. We don't want anybody, I tell you, who isn't capable of some sort of heroism. The revolutionary has got to be a hero—an intelligent and disciplined hero. If you don't feel capable of heroism, then we don't want you. Not at any price. You can go and listen to the band in St. James's Park. You can go and admire the uniforms of the sentries outside Horse Guards.[36] Lovely uniforms! And won't the soldiers look handsome when they're shooting us down in the streets! Mowing us down with machine guns because we dare to ask for justice and freedom, because we have the face to ask to be treated like human beings! But if any of you feel that you're capable of living heroically, like real men and women, not like machines and beasts of burden, not like tame sheep and cringing dogs, then stay and be welcome. If you join us, I warn you, you'll be hated, you'll be persecuted, you'll run the risk of prison, perhaps even of death. I don't hide it. On the contrary, I proclaim it. The people we want are the sort of people who won't be put off by the risk; no, the danger will actually attract them. If you don't understand what I mean, then go away; we don't want you. If you do understand, then come: we need all the comrades we can get. *(There is applause.)*

BARMBY: He speaks well, doesn't he?

JOAN: *(With enthusiasm.)* He's wonderful! And, oh dear, how horribly unheroic one's life is! He makes me feel ashamed of myself.

BARMBY: What a loss to the pulpit! That's what I've always said.

JOAN: Oh, shut up, Phil! Why must you always try to make everything seem silly and ridiculous?

BARMBY: My dear, what blasphemy! Are you implying that the pulpit's silly and ridiculous?

JOAN: You meant it to be.

BARMBY: Not at all. I genuinely think they ought to have made him a bishop. *(He lifts his hands trumpet-wise to his mouth and calls.)* Walter! Walter! *(CLOUGH looks round, smiles, makes a gesture of greeting.)* Come down and talk to us!

CLOUGH: *(Shouting back.)* Later! *(He bends down to speak to people who have come crowding up to his platform. In the course of the following scene he climbs down; somebody takes the board with the Communist emblem and marches off with it.)*

BARMBY: You'll like him, I think. Not much manners. But that's on principle, because of his politics. Those are idiotic, of course.

JOAN: What, the politics?

BARMBY: Yes. I've no patience with that kind of pedantic romanticism. Marxism is just a kind of fairy story—but a fairy story told by a professor. *Jack and the Beanstalk* in words of ten syllables. The long words are supposed to make the wish-fulfilments sound like scientific facts.

JOAN: *(Astonished.)* But . . . But I always thought you were a Communist yourself. I mean, I've heard you arguing with Daddy as though you didn't believe in his system.

BARMBY: Of course I don't believe in his system. But is that any reason why I should believe in Walter's system? One's as absurd as the other. *(Changing his tone.)* Oh, what a pity! The lunatic's packing up to go. *(In effect, the LUNATIC has come down from his perch, which he is folding up preparatory to carrying it away.)* One of my favourite characters. He comes here every Sunday. I wish you'd heard him. There's a moment in his discourse when he talks about his enemy the Pope; it's really sublime. *(To the LUNATIC, who is walking out carrying his perch, towards the right.)* Good night, Professor.

LUNATIC: *(Smiling with pleasure.)* Thank you. *(He shakes BARMBY'S hand.)* And you too, my dear young lady. *(He shakes JOAN'S hand.)* Thank you a thousand times.

JOAN: *(Embarrassed.)* Oh, not at all. I mean . . .

LUNATIC: Your sympathy is a great consolation. I don't know

whether you're acquainted with all the details of my unhappy case. If not, I may as well . . . *(He makes as if to set up his perch again.)*

BARMBY: *(Resolutely intervening.)* Well, goodbye, Professor. It's a thousand pities you've got to go. *(He leads him away towards the right.)*

LUNATIC: But I assure you . . .

BARMBY: No, no. We would not think of detaining you. We know how precious your time is.

LUNATIC: *(Pleading.)* Just a moment! Only one little moment!

BARMBY: No, no. We can't have you making such a sacrifice for us. Absolutely not.

LUNATIC: Really . . .

BARMBY: Another time, Professor. And now you must hurry or you'll be late for your appointment. *(Looks at his watch.)* Goodness me! You must fly.

LUNATIC: Must I?

BARMBY: *(Pushing him out.)* As fast as you can possibly go. Goodbye. *(Exit* LUNATIC. BARMBY *turns back to* JOAN.*)* Well, that was rather masterly, I think; don't you?

JOAN: Poor old thing!

BARMBY: *(Offering her one of the green chairs which stand in front of the right hand shrubbery and himself sitting down on another.)* Oh, don't waste your sympathy. He's far happier than we are. It's absurd to feel sorry for the hero of a romantic novel. Keep your pity for the sane. Some people aren't attracted to romantic novels; they're condemned to inhabit reality. And reality is this. *(He makes a comprehensive gesture.)* This dank and melancholy park; this huge black stinking town with all its millions and millions of dull, unhappy, hideous people. The professor lives in a private paradise all his own. How he enjoys being persecuted by the Pope! Really, I envy him. I should love to be slightly dotty. Not too much, of course. Just a tiny bit cracked. *(Enter, from behind the shrubbery,* WALTER CLOUGH.*)* Ah, but here's Walter. Walter, you were magnificent. A loss to the pulpit as I was saying to Joan. Whom, by the way, you don't know. Joan, this is Mr. Walter Clough. Miss Joan Lidgate. *(They shake hands.)* Yes, Walter, simply magnificent.

CLOUGH: Oh, shut up.

BARMBY: We came, I admit, to mock. But we stayed to pray.[37] Didn't we, Joan?

JOAN: Honestly, Mr. Clough, I did think it was awfully fine, the end of your speech. That was all we heard. I wish we'd been in time for the rest.

CLOUGH: *(Laughing rather grimly.)* I don't know that you'd have enjoyed it much. You're the daughter of Arthur Lidgate, aren't you? *(She nods.)* I hadn't been too complimentary about your father and his friends. *(To BARMBY.)* I hear you're his secretary now.

BARMBY: No, not secretary, exactly. Court fool.

CLOUGH: *(Laughing.)* Typical Barmbyism! I see you haven't changed, Philip. Have you noticed that trick of his, Miss Lidgate? That trick of anticipating any criticism you might make by calling himself all the bad names that he thinks you're going to bestow on him?

JOAN: Well, I've noticed he doesn't seem to have a very high opinion of himself.

CLOUGH: That's where you're wrong. He has an immensely high opinion of himself. So damned high that he can't bear to listen to criticism. That's why he's always running himself down. If you say hard things about yourself, people take your side against you. They're forced to pay you compliments in order to make up for your own unkindness to yourself. It's a very clever trick, really. But then our friend, Philip Barmby, is a very clever man.

BARMBY: Go on, go on. Don't bother about me.

CLOUGH: Oh, I assure you, I'm not bothering about you.

BARMBY: *(Looking at his watch and getting up.)* Anyhow, I've got to go in a moment, I'm afraid.

CLOUGH: You see, Miss Lidgate, he's always looking for excuses and justifications. Justifications for living as he does. Excuses for not doing what he ought to do.

JOAN: What do you think he ought to do?

BARMBY: Join the Communist Party, of course.

CLOUGH: Not that, necessarily. All I ask is that a man should put his money on something. I've no patience with people who want to make the best of both worlds. Either you're too brainless to criticize the present system; in which case you're perfectly justified in conforming to it. Or else you have the intelligence to criticize; in which case it's your duty to act in accordance with your thoughts. To criticize and then do nothing—that's just mental self-indulgence and moral cowardice. *(While he is speaking these last words the* SINGERS *have begun a new hymn.)*

SINGERS: Soldiers of Christ, arise,
And put your armour on,
Strong in the strength which God supplies
Through his eternal Son.[38]

BARMBY: *(Singing softly and beating time as he does so.)* "Soldiers of Christ, arise, and put your armour on." *(To* JOAN, *still beating time while he speaks.)* Joan, I'm going to desert you. Do you mind? *(*JOAN *shakes her head.)* I have to drink tea with my aunts. It's one of the horrors of the sabbath day. *(To* CLOUGH.*)* You'd like me to go and play that harmonium, I suppose.

CLOUGH: There you go again: wriggling out under cover of a joke. But, I tell you, Phil, I respect these old creatures, in spite of their idiocy. At least they don't mind making fools of themselves in public. They've got the courage of their convictions—you haven't.

BARMBY: For the good reason that I have no convictions. You've got to be pretty stupid to have convictions—and stupidity isn't my strong point, I'm afraid.[39]

CLOUGH: Hence you're perfectly justified in doing nothing but sit and smoke Arthur Lidgate's cigars and drink his brandy.

BARMBY: Which aren't, incidentally, nearly so good as you think they are, or as, indeed, they should be. Well, *au revoir mes amis.* Mustn't keep the aunts waiting for their tea. *(He hurries out.)*

JOAN: *Au revoir.*

CLOUGH: You ought to have laughed, you know.

JOAN: What at?

CLOUGH: The joke about your father's brandy and cigars. That was a bit of Phil's famous cynicism.

JOAN: Does he expect one to laugh at that sort of thing? I find it only makes me sad.

CLOUGH: Sad? It puts me in a rage. I hate cynicism. It's the basest way of saying yes to the world as it is. I don't mind the people who say yes, because they genuinely think the world's a nice comfortable place. But the people who know that the world's a pigsty and accept the sty and go and glory in their swinish acceptance—no, those I can't stand. In so far as Phil is one of those people, I really hate him.

JOAN: And yet he's nice.

CLOUGH: Oh, I know. I hate him, but I'm also fond of him.

JOAN: I wish you didn't hate my father.

CLOUGH: I don't; I only hate what he stands for.

JOAN: So do I really.

CLOUGH: *(Smiling.)* Do you?

JOAN: *(Not noticing the smile, very serious.)* Yes, I really hate all that horrible money-grubbing business. It's awful when a nice person stands for something bad.

CLOUGH: And it's equally awful when a beastly person stands for something good. You've got to get used to both of those things if you're a working revolutionary.

JOAN: If only it were possible to make all the beastly people stand for all the beastly things!

CLOUGH: Yes, that *would* simplify matters.

JOAN: One wouldn't mind throwing bombs then.

CLOUGH: Wouldn't one? Bombs are pretty messy, you know.

JOAN: Yes, of course one would mind really. But it would be easier.

If all financiers were like Sir Thomas Lupton, for example. Do you know him? Ugh! But some are like my father. What is one to do?

CLOUGH: One's got to go on making the revolution all the same.

JOAN: I believe you'd get on well with my father.

CLOUGH: Quite probably.

JOAN: He's rather like you, in a way. He's got a lot of life and power—the same as you. Only I wish he used them the way you do. It seems such a waste, spending all that power just to make a lot of money. Why? So that we can live in Monmouth House. But who wants to live in Monmouth House anyhow? *(She sighs. There is a silence.)* You know, I can't help thinking of your speech.

CLOUGH: *(Smiling.)* Can't you? You should try.

JOAN: But I like thinking of it. It was a wonderful speech.

CLOUGH: *Merci, mademoiselle.*

JOAN: No, don't laugh. That's like Phil. I'm serious. It *was* a wonderful speech. At any rate, it was for me. It made all sorts of vague feelings suddenly come clear and definite in my mind. It made me understand things about myself—things I'd never properly realized before. *(Pause.)* I want you to tell me something: what would you do, if you were me?

CLOUGH: If I were you? But I don't know what you are.

JOAN: Well, look at me. You'll see soon enough. *(They look at one another for a moment, then, overcome by a sudden embarrassment, drop their eyes.* JOAN *laughs nervously.)* Not much to see, I'm afraid. Young; silly; fairly pretty; disgustingly rich. What *would* you do?

CLOUGH: What you're doing, I suppose. I'd enjoy myself.

JOAN: I'm not enjoying myself. Not really. Not under the surface. Underneath I really loathe it all. Just how much I loathe it, I only realized this moment, while you were speaking. Loathe the whole silly business, and myself into the bargain.

CLOUGH: That's bad. You mustn't loathe yourself.

JOAN: But I deserve to be loathed. Or perhaps I don't even de-

serve that—only to be despised. You can't loathe futility; it's merely
contemptible. And people won't understand when I tell them it's all
futile. Not even my father. What *shall* I do?

CLOUGH: Why do you expect *me* to know?

JOAN: Well, it's difficult to say. Somehow I feel . . . I feel as though
you had some kind of authority. The way you spoke to that crowd
about being heroic. And the things you said to old Phil. And then, after
all, in a way, you're responsible.

CLOUGH: Me?

JOAN: You brought it all to a head. If I hadn't listened to your
speech . . .

CLOUGH: It wasn't my speech; it was the way you happened to
react to it.

JOAN: No, no; you can't get out of it like that. You may not want
to admit it; but you *are* responsible. Whether you like it or not. That's
why you've got to help me. What *do* you think I ought to do?

(Enter from the left, during the latter part of this speech, the DUKE OF
MONMOUTH. *He dodges round a perambulator, collides with an old lady;
then at last catches sight of* JOAN. *He hurries up to where she is sitting.)*

MONMOUTH: Joan darling! Found at last. They told me at the
house you were supposed to be here. I've been hunting for the last half
hour. My dear, the Church Armies and the anarchists! Deafening! And
what innumerable *canaille!* One will probably be covered with fleas this
evening. Why on earth did you come to this ghastly place?

JOAN: *(Annoyed.)* Because I like the company. *(To* CLOUGH.*)* By
the way, I don't suppose you know one another. Mr. Clough, this is
the Duke of Monmouth. He writes the gossip for the *Daily Gazette*[40]
and we live in his house. *(*CLOUGH *gets up and after shaking hands with*
MONMOUTH *turns to* JOAN.*)*

CLOUGH: Perhaps I'd better be going.

JOAN: No, don't. *Please* don't. *(She catches his sleeve.)* What did
you want, Ted?

MONMOUTH: I'll tell you. You know little Joey Goldberg—*(*JOAN *shakes her head.)* Yes, that American creature I was talking to you about the other day, the one who's so frightfully rich—well, he's giving a party this evening.

JOAN: Well, I'm afraid that doesn't interest me very much.

MONMOUTH: But it's going to be a marvellous party. It's fancy dress, to start with; everyone's got to go either in white or scarlet. And then Joey has taken one of those enormous empty houses in Park Lane—just for this one night.[41] There's going to be hide and seek in the dark. And of course, rivers of champagne. It'll be no end of fun. Joey asked me to dine with him first, and I promised I'd bring you along. Perhaps we ought to go at once and concoct our dresses. Peggy said she was just going to paint herself with lipstick and that's all. But I think you ought to go in white. I'll tell you what I'd thought of for you. White shoes and socks, white shorts, and . . .

JOAN: But I haven't the faintest intention of going to this party.

MONMOUTH: You mean, you've got another engagement?

JOAN: I don't mean anything of the sort. I mean I'm not going.

MONMOUTH: But it's going to be such a divine party!

JOAN: I don't doubt it.

MONMOUTH: I'm having a photographer sent round from the *Gazette.*

JOAN: I should have several photographers.

MONMOUTH: Everybody's going to be there.

JOAN: Except me. And now, would you mind going away, Ted? You've interrupted us in the middle of a most interesting conversation.

MONMOUTH: No, but listen here.

JOAN: Goodbye, Ted. *(She holds out her hand.)* And I do hope you'll enjoy yourself. Remember to give my love to Peggy.

MONMOUTH: Joan, Darling . . .

JOAN: *(Peremptorily.)* Goodbye!

MONMOUTH: *(Looks at her, then shrugs his shoulders.)* Oh, very well. *(He goes out.)*

CLOUGH: I'm sorry for that young man.

JOAN: I'm not.

CLOUGH: *(Smiling.)* No, I could see that.

JOAN: You know, I'm so ashamed.

CLOUGH: What about?

JOAN: That party. That disgusting, vulgar, idiotic party.

CLOUGH: I don't know why you should feel ashamed. It wasn't your party.

JOAN: It was my sort of party. After all, I was going to it.

CLOUGH: You weren't.

JOAN: No, but I probably should have if I hadn't met you. Oh, it's too stupid and revolting! But you see what I've got to put up with.

CLOUGH: Yes, I see.

JOAN: And you say that people ought to live heroically. Living heroically at Joey Goldberg's parties! *(Turning on him almost fiercely.)* Oh, why don't you tell me what I ought to do? *(They look at one another without speaking. The sound of the hymn swells louder, and the* CURTAIN *comes down.)*

Act II

Scene 2

The Library at Monmouth House six weeks later. LIDGATE *and* BARMBY *are sitting in front of the fire.* BARMBY *holds a book in his hand and is reading aloud.*

BARMBY: Darkling, I listen; and, for many a time
I have been half in love with easeful Death,
Called him soft names in many a musèd rhyme,
To take into the air my quiet breath;
Now more than ever seems it rich to die,
To cease upon the midnight with no pain,
While thou art pouring forth thy soul abroad
  In such an ecstasy.
Still wouldst thou sing, and I have ears in vain—
To thy high requiem become a sod.

LIDGATE: I say, that's wonderful. May I just look? *(Takes the book from* BARMBY.*)* "Now more than ever seems it rich to die, / To cease upon the midnight with no pain." Curious; I've often felt like that. How extraordinarily *comfortable* it would be. One gets so damnably tired sometimes. "Darkling, I listen; and, for many a time / I have been half in love with easeful Death." Yes, *"easeful."* He gets it exactly. Just what I feel, only more so, if you see what I mean.

BARMBY: That's what all good art does—says just what you feel, only much more so. Whereas bad art says just what you feel only less so—all that you feel when you're at your worst and stupidest and laziest. Imagine how Ella Wheeler Wilcox[42] would have written the "Ode to a Nightingale!"

LIDGATE: By the way, who *did* write it actually? *(He looks at the title page of the book.)* Oh, of course, John Keats. "Ode to a Nightingale" by John Keats. I must remember that. "Ode to a Nightingale" by John Keats.[43] But now tell me something, Barmby. You talk about good art and bad art. But how does one know which is which?

43

BARMBY: Well, of course, most people don't know. Even quite intelligent, well-educated people. You've got to be one of the few who happen to be born with the right kind of perceptions.

LIDGATE: That isn't very encouraging for me, is it?

BARMBY: No, it isn't. But then how few things *are* encouraging!

LIDGATE: *(With a little mirthless laugh.)* Yes, my God, how few! And yet for some reason one goes on. This accursed iron and steel business of mine, for example. I go on and on, and the load grows heavier and heavier, and the way more and more difficult to find. I don't know why the hell one doesn't just sit back and take things easy. But it seems impossible.

BARMBY: Impossible for you. But, thank heaven, not for me. *(He settles more deeply in his chair, and lights a cigarette.)* I find no difficulty in sitting back.

LIDGATE: I suppose it's a question of temperament.

BARMBY: Just a matter of the ductless glands, that's all. Mine happen to be more than averagely ductless. Almost hermetically sealed.

LIDGATE: *(Laughing.)* I wish mine were. *(In another tone.)* Oh dear! *(He draws his hand wearily across his forehead; then gets up and walks in a nervous preoccupied way to the fireplace, where he stands, leaning against the mantelpiece.)* There's another thing that's been on my mind lately. I wanted to ask you about it, Barmby. I'm rather worried about Joan. She seems to be so restless and dissatisfied.

BARMBY: She happens to be her father's daughter.

LIDGATE: What do you mean?

BARMBY: She doesn't know how to sit back. And you're trying to make her lead a life that consists of nothing but sitting back.

LIDGATE: I only want her to be happy, to have a good time.

BARMBY: I know; but unfortunately she's one of those people who are only happy when they're giving themselves a bad time. Only she hasn't got any worries yet. She's still looking for them.

LIDGATE: I'm ready to let her do whatever she likes.

BARMBY: But she doesn't want to do what she likes. She wants to do what somebody else likes.

LIDGATE: Somebody else? But who?

BARMBY: Ah, that's just the question. It might be St. Francis of Assisi. Or, on the contrary, it might be Sir Oswald Mosley.[44] Or again, it might be Karl Marx. My own guess is that it'll be a mixture of Karl Marx and St. Francis.

LIDGATE: What makes you think that?

BARMBY: Oh . . . masculine intuition, I suppose.

(During the latter part of this dialogue, SPENCE *comes into the room and stands waiting for an opportunity to speak to* LIDGATE.*)*

SPENCE: These letters have just come in, Mr. Lidgate. And your evening call to New York is coming through this moment.

LIDGATE: Damn! Put the letters down on the table, will you. Sorry, Barmby. I'll be back in a minute.

BARMBY: *(To* LIDGATE, *as he goes out.)* Don't hurry. Culture can wait. It's used to waiting. Isn't it, Mr. Spence.

SPENCE: Are you trying to make fun of me, Mr. Barmby?

BARMBY: *Me* make fun of *you?*

SPENCE: I tell you frankly, Mr. Barmby, I don't like your attitude.

BARMBY: Nor do I, Mr. Spence. I think my attitude is deplorable. But it would need such an intolerable effort to change it.

SPENCE: All that what's-the-good-of-anything-why-nothing kind of talk of yours—it's wrong, I tell you. And the way you take it upon yourself to criticize everything and everyone. Wrong again. You're a young man, Mr. Barmby . . .

BARMBY: Ah, but old in vice, Mr. Spence.

SPENCE: And I'm getting on; I'm nearly sixty. So I feel I have the right to say it. You ought to have more respect, Mr. Barmby. I tell you, a man like you ought to show respect to a man like Mr. Lidgate. Mr. Lidgate's a good man, a high-minded man.

BARMBY: He's certainly a very rich man.

SPENCE: I've worked for him for upwards of twenty years now, and I know him. There isn't a finer man in the country, I tell you. There isn't anyone more deserving of respect. And I want you to know it, Mr. Barmby. I want you to realize who you're dealing with. I tell you I don't like your disrespectful manner towards him.

BARMBY: No, I can see you wouldn't, Mr. Spence. After twenty years—obviously, you'd hate it. *(JOAN'S voice is heard off saying, "And this is the library." The door opens and she comes in followed by* CLOUGH.*)* Hullo!

JOAN: Oh, Hullo, Phil. I was just showing Walter the house.

BARMBY: So he's actually consented to set foot in the enemy's camp. Well, well! I congratulate you, Joan.

JOAN: *(Annoyed.)* Oh, don't be a fool, Philip.

CLOUGH: *(With studied detachment.)* It's a lovely house. I've always been very fond of this late eighteenth-century stuff.

BARMBY: Have you, indeed? Well, isn't that curious! So have I. Ever since the age of puberty. *(Getting up.)* Let me do the honours. *(He takes* CLOUGH'S *arm and leads him to one of the portraits. Their conversation becomes momentarily inaudible.)*

JOAN: Well, Mr. Spence.

SPENCE: Good evening, Miss Joan.

JOAN: How's your sister, Mr. Spence?

SPENCE: Oh, she's moderately well, thank you, Miss Joan. The lumbago's better. But she's having a good deal of trouble with her acidity.

JOAN: Oh dear!

SPENCE: She can't touch anything fried. Simply can't touch it. The doctor was saying to me only yesterday, "Mr. Spence," he says, "she might as well eat weed killer as fried potatoes." *(The conversation continues unheard, while the others carry on the dialogue.)*

CLOUGH: *(Looking round him.)* My word, these Adam brothers knew how to make a fine room, didn't they![45]

BARMBY: And what a library! *(He pats the backs of the nearest books.)* Why anyone should take to drink or opium when there are all these lovely books in the world, I really can't imagine. Reading's so incomparably the pleasantest vice to wallow in.

CLOUGH: I wish I could do a bit of wallowing for a change. *(He takes out a volume, opens it and turns over the pages, lovingly.)*

BARMBY: Well, wallow. Don't be such a puritan. I've no patience with a man who deliberately mortifies his soul with Karl Marx and statistics, when he might be reading real books.

CLOUGH: And I have no patience with a man who wastes his time indulging in literature, when he ought to be thinking how to make the world fit for human beings to live in. *(Puts the book back in its place with symbolic emphasis.)*

BARMBY: But if you're the right sort of human being in the right sort of social position, I assure you, the world is perfectly fit to live in. I find it absolutely delightful; it might have been specially made for me.

CLOUGH: Now, don't start showing off your bad qualities. It doesn't make them any more excusable. On the contrary, it makes them less excusable. "Forgive them for they know not what they do." [46] But if they do know what they do, and not only know but boast about their knowledge, then there can be no forgiveness. You can't even forgive yourself.

BARMBY: Quite true: you can't. But I find I can get on quite happily without my own forgiveness. *(To JOAN.)* Joan!

JOAN: Yes?

BARMBY: It may amuse you to hear that I'm making your father read Keats.

JOAN: Poor lamb! Does he mind?

BARMBY: No, he seems to like it—fairly laps up the culture. Doesn't he, Mr. Spence?

SPENCE: It all seems a lot of nonsense to me. What does he want with all this stuff? What has it got to do with his work?

BARMBY: Nothing whatever. If it had, it wouldn't be culture.

SPENCE: Well, if that's so then I think he'd do better to mind his own business. However, it isn't my place to criticize. I must get back to my work. Good evening, Miss Joan.

JOAN: Good evening, Mr. Spence. *(As he opens the door to go out,* SPENCE *runs into* LIDGATE *returning.)*

SPENCE: Oh, I beg your pardon, Mr. Lidgate.

LIDGATE: I'll call you down when I've looked at those letters, Spence.

SPENCE: Very good, sir. *(He goes out.)*

LIDGATE: *(His face lighting up as he sees* JOAN.*)* Oh, you're here, are you? *(He kisses her.)*

JOAN: You don't mind?

LIDGATE: *(Affectionately.)* Mind? I'm furious. *(Going over to the writing table.)* I was wanting to see you, as a matter of fact. I've got a little surprise for you here. *(He has not noticed* CLOUGH, *who is standing with* BARMBY *in a corner.)* Where is it now? *(He opens a drawer and searches.)*

JOAN: This is Mr. Clough, by the way. I was just showing him round the house. *(*CLOUGH *comes forward.)* He's very much interested in architecture.

BARMBY: *(In a whisper.)* Late eighteenth-century architecture.

LIDGATE: *(Has found what he was looking for—a green leather case. At* JOAN'S *words, he turns round, surprised; he shakes hands with* CLOUGH.*)* Still more interested in economics, if I'm not mistaken. Aren't you the Walter Clough who wrote those articles in the *Daily Masses?*[47]

CLOUGH: I'm afraid I am.

LIDGATE: They weren't very kind.

CLOUGH: They were only meant to be true.

LIDGATE: Well, they weren't even that. A lot of your facts were wrong. And then, you know, I'm not quite such a monster as you make out. Am I, Joan?

JOAN: *(Distressed.)* But Walter wasn't ever saying anything personal. You mustn't imagine that. Really, Daddy. It's the system he's attacking. If the system were changed . . .

BARMBY: . . . he'd be a monster of another kind.

JOAN: Oh, be quiet, Phil!

BARMBY: A tyrannical bureaucrat instead of a tyrannical plutocrat. And what a huge improvement *that* would be!

JOAN: No, but seriously, Daddy, you mustn't think that Walter . . .

LIDGATE: *(Putting his arm round her.)* But, my dear, I don't think. And even if I did, it really wouldn't upset me. I'm used to being called names. Extravagantly good names as well as extravagantly bad names. Every rich man gets called them. I don't pay much attention to either kind.

JOAN: Well, I'm glad of that. *(She presses herself affectionately against him. Then looks up, as a new thought crosses her mind, with a serious expression.)* Though I *do* think you ought to pay attention to Walter's arguments, I mean, if he can *prove* that your system is wrong . . .

LIDGATE: *(Laughing.)* You and your systems! *(He pats her shoulder.)*

JOAN: No, don't laugh.

LIDGATE: I can't help it.

JOAN: You don't take me seriously.

LIDGATE: No, I confess I don't. But now look at this. Here's the little surprise I wanted to show you. *(He opens the case and pulls out a necklace of pearls and emeralds.)* What do you think of that? *(JOAN examines it in silence.* BARMBY *approaches and looks at it over her shoulder.)*

BARMBY: Pearls? I must say, they're large enough. *(To* LIDGATE.*)* Oyster or Woolworth?

LIDGATE: Woolworth, indeed! This belonged to the Russian royal family. There was a whole mass of their stuff being sold this afternoon at Christies.[48] Fantastic! Like stage jewels. Quite unwearable most of them. Try it on, Joan.

JOAN: But is it . . . is it meant for me, Daddy?

LIDGATE: Who do you suppose it's meant for? Spence? Now then, let's try it on. I want to see how it suits you.

JOAN: But, Daddy, I couldn't. Really. Oh, you oughtn't to have got it for me.

LIDGATE: But don't you like it? I thought . . . Well, it seemed to me so pretty, the white and green together, like this.

JOAN: I'm so miserable.

LIDGATE: Joan, darling . . .

JOAN: You've been so sweet—and now I shall seem such a beast— so ungrateful. But, Daddy, I can't take it. I don't *want* it.

LIDGATE: But why not, Joan?

JOAN: I should feel so frightfully guilty, if I took it. When you think of all the people who haven't got enough to eat. It would be like hitting them in the face. And then—that's not all—then . . . Well, can't you understand? I don't want to be just rich and silly and selfish. I don't want to be always taking things; taking, taking, taking, and never giving anything at all. I want to pay for things; you know, really *pay*—not just with money; with my own efforts. Don't you understand, Daddy? Oh dear, I can't explain. And it all sounds so horribly stupid and priggish. I can't talk about it. Not now. *(Her voice trembles on the verge of tears.)* Here, Daddy. Take it. *(She hands him the necklace.)* I'm sorry. I'm being stupid. I think I'd better go away. *(She hurries towards the door, crying. There is a long silence. Slowly and methodically,* LIDGATE *puts the necklace back into its case and the case into the drawer.)*

BARMBY: *(Overacting the easy, natural, unembarrassed manner.)* Well, if you don't need me any more this evening, Mr. Lidgate . . .

LIDGATE: *(Says nothing for a few seconds; then, giving himself a little shake, sits down briskly at the writing table and picks up the sheaf of letters left by* SPENCE.*)* No, I've got my letters to do now, Barmby.

BARMBY: Well, in that case, Walter, I think we'd better be going.

CLOUGH: All right. *(He goes up to the table.)* Goodbye, Mr. Lidgate.

LIDGATE: *(Looks at him for a few seconds without speaking and with-*

out making any movement to take CLOUGH'S *outstretched hand. When he speaks, it is in a very low voice, that trembles with suppressed fury.)* Don't ever come to this house again. Do you understand? *(Breaking out with sudden loud violence and striking the table with his fist.)* I won't have it. Do you hear? I won't have it. *(Controlling himself again, and speaking once more in a low voice.)* Go now. Go quickly. *(He picks up the letters once more and makes as though he were deeply absorbed in the reading of them.* CLOUGH *stands for a moment, uncertain whether to answer or not; then shrugs his shoulders and walks towards the door. He and* BARMBY *go out together.* LIDGATE *picks up a pen and writes a note in the margin of the first letter, blots it and puts it into the tray on his left. Then he gets up, walks restlessly to the fireplace and stands there, his elbows on the mantelpiece, his face in his hands. After a few seconds, he returns to the writing table, picks up the house telephone, dials, rings.)* That you, Spence? Come down to the library, will you. *(He replaces the receiver and goes on with his reading and annotating. Enter* SPENCE, *who stands near the table, waiting for* LIDGATE *to look up.* LIDGATE *makes a last note, then turns to his secretary.)* It's about those municipal loans, Spence. I've got the exact wording and lay-out for the bonds. Where the devil is it? *(He rummages in a drawer and at last produces a sheet of paper.)* Ah, here we are! I think that's quite O.K. now. You can take it down to the printers tomorrow.

SPENCE: How many copies shall I get them to print, sir?

LIDGATE: Why, as many as make up the issue. The Coventry loan's for a million and a half and the bonds are for ten thousand each; so we shall need a hundred and fifty. And a hundred and seventy-five for Portsmouth. And two hundred for Nottingham.

SPENCE: Very well. Is there anything else, sir?

LIDGATE: Yes, these letters you brought me. *(He hands him papers.)* I've made notes in the margin. You see. *(He shows him on the letters.)* "No." "Send details." "Renew for two months." "Go to hell." And so on. I leave you to concoct the rest.

SPENCE: Very good, sir. I think I can manage.

LIDGATE: Much better than I. I never could write a good letter. Not like one of yours, Spence.

SPENCE: *(Delighted by the praise.)* What nonsense, sir!

LIDGATE: I often wonder where I should be without you, Spence! Certainly in Carey Street; probably in quod.[49] *(He sighs, and stretches himself wearily.)* Well, anyhow it would be nice and restful in either place. "Now more than ever seems it rich . . ."

SPENCE: I beg your pardon, sir?

LIDGATE: Oh, nothing; just a line of poetry.

SPENCE: What you need is a good holiday, sir.

LIDGATE: I know I do. But I can't take one before this damned iron and steel business is settled. By the by, Lupton said he was coming in this evening. I wish I could make out why he's started all this shilly-shallying again. It all seemed settled with Wertheim's and now . . . Goodness knows. I'm sorry now I put so much reliance on him. I could have fixed up something in some other quarter. But now it's too late. When is it exactly that my option expires?

SPENCE: Wednesday of next week, sir. Payment to be completed within twenty days of that date.

LIDGATE: And Lupton still refuses to say anything definite, damn him?

SPENCE: Shall I tell you my private opinion, sir?

LIDGATE: What is it?

SPENCE: He's after the game on his own account.

LIDGATE: What do you mean?

SPENCE: Why, don't you see, sir? He'd like you to drop your option so that he could take it up himself. And with Wertheim's behind him—well, obviously, he'd have no difficulty.

LIDGATE: Do you think that's what he's really working for?

SPENCE: I'm sure of it, Mr. Lidgate. But hadn't you guessed, sir?

LIDGATE: *(Agitatedly walking up and down the room.)* No, it never occurred to me. I'd somehow got it into my head that the whole thing was fixed. In spite of all these shifty tricks of his. *(Pause.)* But what does he want to do with his iron and steel when he gets it? You don't see Lupton taking the trouble to re-organize an industry. He's only a speculator.

SPENCE: Well, that's just what he's doing, sir—speculating. He'll push up the shares—the news of the amalgamation will send them up even without his pushing—and then he'll clear out at a profit.

LIDGATE: Leaving the industry worse off than it was before. *(With sudden vehemence. His fatigue has vanished.)* No, that can't be allowed; that simply can't be allowed.

SPENCE: It certainly oughtn't to be allowed, sir. But if he's got all the cards in his hand—and all the money in his pocket . . .

FOOTMAN: *(Opens the door and announces.)* Sir Thomas Lupton. *(Enter* LUPTON.*)*

LUPTON: *(Very genial.)* Well, Arthur, my lad, and how are you? Bearing up in spite of the weather? Evening, Spence.

SPENCE: Good evening, Sir Thomas.

LUPTON: *(Helping himself from the bottle on the table near the fire.)* I'll help myself to a spot of gin, if I may, Arthur. Just to drive the fog out of me. Well, cheerio! *(He drinks.)* What a ghastly climate! My constitution won't stand it. I'm thinking of running down to Monte Carlo for a bit at the end of next week.

LIDGATE: When you've fixed up your little deal with the iron and steel people, eh?

LUPTON: *(Taken aback.)* My little deal with . . . Who says I'm having a deal with them? I . . . I'm not having anything of the kind.

LIDGATE: *(To* SPENCE.*)* Yes, you were quite right, Spence. My God what a fool I've been!

LUPTON: What the devil are you talking about, Lidgate?

LIDGATE: I'm talking about your little scheme for robbing me of all the results of my work. That's all.

LUPTON: But, my dear chap, you're mad; I don't know what you mean.

LIDGATE: You *do* know what I mean; and I'm not your dear chap. Your plan was to keep me uncertain about Wertheim's up to the very last moment; then, just as my option was expiring, you meant to tell me that they couldn't advance the money. Then I'd have had to abandon the option and you'd have stepped into my place with Wertheim's cheque in your pocket. Wasn't that it? Well, let me tell you straight away: you're damned well not going to be given the chance. I'm taking up the option in any case whatever Wertheim's decision may be.

SPENCE: What, sir? Do you mean to say . . . ?

LIDGATE: Kindly don't interrupt me, Spence.

SPENCE: I beg your pardon, Mr. Lidgate.

LIDGATE: If Wertheim's let me down at the last moment—and evidently that's what you've advised them to do—well, they're not the only people with capital. I shall go somewhere else—and so much the worse for Wertheim's.

LUPTON: You'll find it precious difficult to raise the money.

LIDGATE: Oh, you've made it inconvenient for me: I'm ready to admit it. But you can't put me off with a little inconvenience. I should have thought you knew me well enough to realize that, Lupton.

LUPTON: Now, look here, old man, don't let's misunderstand one another.

LIDGATE: But I assure you, I don't misunderstand you. On the contrary, I understand you only too well. You want to play a dirty trick on me. Well, it's only natural in you; I ought to have known it from the first. But I don't want to have dirty tricks played on me. That's also natural.

LUPTON: You know, I believe I could persuade old Wertheim to change his mind.

LIDGATE: Yes, and change it again next Wednesday, five minutes before I sign the agreement. No thank you. I'm doing this business on my own now. Whatever it costs. I'm damned if I'm going to allow you and Wertheim to play the fool with a whole industry. All you want to do is gamble with it—gamble with the lives of hundreds of thousands of decent men and women. It's not good enough. Go to your Monte Carlo if you want to gamble. You shan't do it here. Not if I can help it.

Act III

Scene 1

Time, a month later; place, CLOUGH'S *living room. It is a small bare room, colour-washed, with linoleum on the floor. A black Victorian fireplace on the left holds a gas fire. Placed, slantingly in front of it, is a rugged old sofa. There is one table, with tea things on it, in the middle of the room and another, covered with books and papers, against the back wall, between the windows. The door is on the right. There are bookshelves on each side of the fireplace. The only pictures are a photogravure of Lenin and a reproduction of a Cézanne landscape, over the mantelpiece. A small piano, a cupboard and three or four kitchen chairs, make up the rest of the furniture.* JOAN *is sitting, almost lying, on the sofa, her hands under her head.* CLOUGH *is squatting down on one side of the fireplace, engaged in putting coins into the gas meter.*

CLOUGH: ... four, five, six, seven. *(He puts pennies into the slot and, after each insertion, turns the handle; the coins fall rattling into the meter. He dives into his waistcoat pockets for more pennies.)* I say, I do apologize for this sofa. *(With his free hand he pulls out a wisp of stuffing from a hole in the cover.)*

JOAN: But it's comfortable. Which is all that matters.

CLOUGH: *(Looking at her admiringly.)* I wish I knew how to draw. *(He traces a line through the air with his finger.)*

JOAN: Oh, dear, I know what that means. *(She straightens herself up.)* It means I'm not sitting in a ladylike position. Is that better? *(She makes a pretence to be primly rigid.)*

CLOUGH: *(Looks at her a moment in silence, then sighs.)* Yes, alas it is. Much better. *(He brings the hand out of his pocket with several more pennies.)* Let's see, how many had I put in? Seven, wasn't it? Eight. Nine, ten, eleven. Well, that'll keep us warm for an hour or two.

JOAN: It seems awfully inconvenient with all those pennies. Why don't you have your meter arranged so that you can pay once a quarter?

57

CLOUGH: Because the gas company wouldn't trust me. The poor don't get any credit. They have to pay on the nail—preferably in advance. *You* could get free gas for a year, if you wanted to.

JOAN: You needn't throw it in my teeth like that. How beastly you are, sometimes, Walter!

CLOUGH: Am I, Joan? *(He laughs sadly.)* I wish I could afford not to be. *(He takes her hand, and very quickly kisses it.)* God, how I should enjoy doing all kinds of things I can't afford! *(Quickly changing the subject.)* More tea, Joan? Bread and butter? Buns?

JOAN: No thanks.

CLOUGH: Cigarette, then?

JOAN: All right, I'll smoke one of your disgusting gaspers. Just to mortify the flesh. *(She lights the cigarette.)* Pugh! *(She makes a face.)* I believe you get a lot of fun really out of your asceticism don't you, Walter? More than poor old Philip gets out of his cigars and brandy?

CLOUGH: More? No. I get a different kind of fun. A better kind, I should say. But then I'm probably prejudiced.

JOAN: Did you mind much when you started giving things up?

CLOUGH: Well, there were some things that needed a bit of effort. Getting up early on winter mornings—I don't think I shall ever be fully reconciled to that.

JOAN: Poor Walter! Couldn't you make an exception for late breakfast?

CLOUGH: No, no, that wouldn't be playing the game. One's got no right to shirk something that other people have got to put up with.

JOAN: But most people do shirk, all the same. Look at me, for example. I wish I had your strength of mind, Walter.

CLOUGH: It doesn't need much strength of mind. Only strength of conviction. You've got to be convinced of the value of the cause. Then it's easy to make sacrifices for it.

JOAN: Easy, if there's nobody to consider but yourself. You never had someone standing in your way—someone you cared for as much as I care for Daddy. Oh dear, why must one always be hurting people?

CLOUGH: Because they're hurtable. It can't be helped.

JOAN: It's horrible. I only want to do what I feel is right and decent —and it makes poor Daddy unutterably wretched. And if it makes him wretched, is it still right and decent?

CLOUGH: Yes, it is.

JOAN: Oh, it's easy enough to say that when he's not there. But when I see him being unhappy . . . Oh dear! *(She shakes her head.)* And perhaps, after all, it's only an excuse for my own cowardice. Perhaps I secretly feel I should regret giving it all up—all the comfortable privileges.

CLOUGH: Yes, you've got a lot to give up. Luckily, I never had as many privileges as you have.

JOAN: You only had the real privileges—the ones that can't be given up: your mind, your talents, your will. You know, when one comes to think of it, it is most frightfully unfair that some people should be—well—almost like dogs, so far as intelligence goes, while others should be Einstein, and Shakespeare, and Napoleon. People who are strong and intelligent are shirking something that the majority of us have to put up with. If you were really consistent, Walter, you'd try to make yourself stupid and feeble.

CLOUGH: But, luckily or unluckily, one isn't consistent. If I were consistent, I shouldn't be . . . *(He breaks off, and gets up. All through this scene he has been looking at* JOAN, *and it is obvious that he is a man deeply in love, controlling his passion. He walks restlessly about the room.)*

JOAN: You wouldn't be doing what?

CLOUGH: *(Shaking his head.)* Oh, nothing. *(There is a silence. He suddenly turns towards* JOAN.*)* Do you know what I've always found the most difficult thing?

JOAN: Do you mean, the most difficult to give up?

CLOUGH: No, no. Giving up things is really not difficult at all. Even one's independence. I don't like obeying—particularly people I think stupider than I am. But I'm ready to do it for the sake of the cause. That isn't really difficult.

JOAN: What is difficult, then?

CLOUGH: I'll tell you. The real difficulty is loving the men and women one's trying to help. That Christian insistence on love—I used to think it was all rather silly and sentimental. But I see now I was wrong. Loving one's neighbour is heroic. Heroic because it's so damnably difficult, the most difficult thing in the world. I've never been able to do it.

JOAN: But if you don't love your neighbour, why do you make sacrifices for him?

CLOUGH: Because I hate injustice, I hate the criminal stupidity and insensitiveness of the people who perpetrate the injustice. But as for saying that I love the men and women I want to save from the exploiters—no; it wouldn't be true. I don't. They bore me. They make me impatient. Why are their minds so limited and personal? Always, me, me, you, you: never an idea or a generalisation. And then that awful complacency and indifference and resignation! The way they put up with intolerable situations! Nobody has a right to be resigned to slums and sweated labour and fat men guzzling at the Savoy.[50] But damn them, they *are* resigned. And then I don't enjoy their pleasures. The movies, and jazz, and looking on at football—it bores me stiff—and, of course what *I* call pleasure they detest. It's a case of chronic and fundamental misunderstanding. Which isn't exactly the best foundation for love. But all the same, I believe it is possible to love one's neighbour even though one may have very little in common with him. I believe there's some way of learning to love him. Through humility, perhaps. *(Pause.)* Queer, the way one finds oneself using religious language. But they knew a lot about human beings, those Christians. If only they hadn't used their knowledge to such bad ends. One's got to take the good, and just ruthlessly stamp out the rest. All the disgusting superstitions and the stupid cocksure intolerance. They've got to be fought and conquered and utterly abolished.

JOAN: Don't you wish sometimes that you could abolish everything—the whole world and everyone in it?

CLOUGH: Do I wish it? Good heavens! Do you know what I've got to do tonight? I've got to go to Barcelona for a conference.[51] Four days

now. If you love somebody a lot, it makes a kind of bridge between you and the rest of the world. You know how difficult it is to believe that other people are really there at all. You see them, you shake hands with them. But you never think of them as complete people like yourself. Well, if you love somebody, you do think of him as a complete person. That's what love is. And that opens your eyes to the rest of the world. You suddenly realize that the world's full of people, every one of them as complete and real as you are. And when you've realized that about them, you begin to love them. Listen, Walter, you say you're sad because you can't love everybody. But, I tell you, you can't expect to love everybody till you allow yourself to love somebody. *(Raising his face from her knees, so that she can look into it.)* And you've got to love her terribly much, do you hear? You've got to love her to the very limit, with all your heart and with all your soul. Oh, Walter, say that you love me; say that you love me. *(He looks at her without speaking.)* Why don't you say it? Walter! What are you doing? *(Slowly, without speaking, he disengages her hands, he rises to his feet.)* Walter! Don't you love me?

CLOUGH: I love you too much. I had no right ... I was weak. *(Turning on* JOAN *with a kind of fury.)* Can't you see it's just madness? The idea of you living here with me, feeding pennies into the gas meter. Cooking and washing up. You! It's idiotic, I tell you. You'd be miserable before the week was out. And then your misery would blackmail me into taking your father's beastly money. And I'd consent, because I love you. And that would be the end. I'd love you so much that I'd let myself be dishonoured. And then I'd come to hate you.

JOAN: But, Walter. I wouldn't mind doing those things.

CLOUGH: But you've never tried.

JOAN: But you're insulting me, Walter. You're saying I shouldn't have spirit enough to be able to put up with a little discomfort.

CLOUGH: A little discomfort! But, Joan, you've no conception what poverty is. You'd find it unbearable.

JOAN: How can you love me, then, if you think I'm such a cowardly little fool?

CLOUGH: I don't think so. I just know that you haven't any experience of the sort of life you'd have to lead, if you were to marry me. And I also know what my reactions would be if I saw you being unhappy. I love you too much.

JOAN: But, Walter, I wouldn't want you to give up anything for me. I wouldn't let you.

CLOUGH: I tell you, you don't know what poverty is.

JOAN: Have you so little faith in me, then?

CLOUGH: Not much in myself even. The self that loves you and desires you and needs your tenderness—no, I can't trust it. I'd promised I wouldn't tell you how much I loved you. But just now, when you said that, I was so . . . so moved: it was like heaven, such an unbelievable happiness . . . I broke my promise. And now I've had to hurt you, and hurt myself, and behave like a cad.

JOAN: But, Walter . . .

CLOUGH: No, no. Please. Please go away. It's no good, Joan. We're only hurting one another.

JOAN: *(After a pause, in a very low voice.)* Do you really want me to go?

CLOUGH: *(Who is standing with his back to her, leaning on the mantelpiece, nods his head.)* Yes.

JOAN: *(Puts on her hat, picks up her coat, and moves towards the door. When she is almost at the door, she turns back.)* Walter! *(He makes a little sound, indicating that he is listening.)* I'm going, Walter.

CLOUGH: *(Without looking round.)* Goodbye, Joan.

JOAN: Goodbye. *(She opens the door, then looks round again. He is still standing motionless by the fireplace. She hesitates, then goes out, closing the door behind her. The* CURTAIN *slowly falls.)*

Act III

Scene 2

The same evening in the library at Monmouth House. LIDGATE *is telephoning as the curtain rises.* SPENCE *sits by, pale and fidgeting with apprehension.*

LIDGATE: But that's absurd! What more do they want? . . . But they've advanced me money before on the same sort of security . . . Not so much, I agree. But I'm offering more security this time . . . Oh! I see! . . . What is the *real* reason then? . . . Rumours? What sort of rumours? . . . But that's not true; that's just a lie . . . They're fools to believe such a thing . . . Have you any idea where these rumours started? . . . Ah, I guessed as much! Lupton tried to play a dirty trick on me last month and I caught him in the act. He's trying to take his revenge. Don't they know Lupton well enough by this time? . . . But am I to be put to this inconvenience just because a scoundrel chooses to tell lies about me? . . . Raise the money elsewhere? Yes, of course I can raise it elsewhere. But it's a nuisance. I go to my old friends first because it's easier, because I expect to be treated with consideration. Instead of which, I'm received as though I were a beggar or a crook. It's insulting! . . . Very well then. If that's the case, you can tell them with my compliments that I shall never have any dealings with them again. They've done very well out of me in the past. But after this they shall never get another piece of business from me. Tell them that. Never so long as I live. Good night. *(He hangs up the receiver and turns to* SPENCE, *smiling.)* Always take the high line, Spence. Even when you're low— particularly when you're low. It's a great comfort to be able at least to talk as though you were God Almighty. *(Telephone bell rings.)* Damn that bell! See who it is, Spence.

SPENCE: Hullo? . . . Mr. Lidgate's secretary speaking. Who is it? . . . Oh, good evening Mr. Thompson. One moment. I'll just see if Mr. Lidgate can speak to you. *(To* LIDGATE.) It's Thompson, sir. You know; the manager of Metropolitan Electric.

LIDGATE: Give me the thing. *(He takes the instrument from* SPENCE.*)* Hullo. That you, Thompson? Lidgate speaking. What news of your conference this afternoon? . . . What? The men won't accept our offer? But we had the union leaders' word for it . . . But why's that? . . . They've thrown their leaders over? . . . Agitators going behind the union, I suppose . . . Yes . . . Yes . . . Then you don't think we shall get them back to work this week, as we hoped? . . . Oh, my God! No, of course we couldn't agree to that. Out of the question . . . Yes, you're right. It couldn't have happened at a worse moment. I'm afraid it's killed our chance of getting that contract for the Danish State Railways. Who'd accept a tender from a factory that isn't even working? If we'd been able to get them back today, then there might have been a possibility . . . Oh, I know you're doing your best, Thompson. But circumstances are doing their worst, I'm afraid . . . Quite . . . Quite . . . Goodbye. *(He hangs up the receiver. To* SPENCE.*)* Well, there goes one more forlorn hope. If we could have got the men back, we might have got the contract. And if we'd got the contract, we could have set it off against the overdraft and got back those bonds. As it is the money falls due tomorrow, they'll put the bonds on the market, and then . . . *(He shrugs his shoulders.)*

SPENCE: It's terrible, sir, it's terrible. What are we going to do, sir?

LIDGATE: Why do you ask me, Spence? Do you think I know any better than you? *(He laughs.)* There's something rather comic about a situation from which there's no possible issue.

SPENCE: Oh, if you'd only listened to me, sir! Didn't I tell you from the first that you ought to keep out of it? Didn't I tell you from the first it was all wrong?

LIDGATE: Yes, you did, Spence. And I told *you* from the first that it was less wrong than leaving the business to Lupton and that I was damned well going to stay in. So you see we both had warning, Spence —I from you and you from me.

SPENCE: *(His self-control progressively breaking down as he speaks.)* But what is going to happen, sir? What'll they do when . . . When they find out? This time tomorrow—Oh, I daren't think of it, Mr. Lidgate.

I daren't think of it; but the thought's always there—like a clock inside my head. "Tomorrow, tomorrow, tomorrow"—over and over again. And, each time, tomorrow's a little bit nearer. It's driving me crazy, sir. I can't stand it. I can't stand the feeling that I've done something wrong. I'd never done anything before that wasn't right. Not in all my life. It makes me suddenly feel as if I were all alone. As if everyone were against me. Why didn't you take my advice, sir? I told you it wasn't right. I told you. And tomorrow they'll come, they'll come and take us, take us away . . . No, I can't stand it, Mr. Lidgate, I can't stand it. *(He covers his face with his hands.)*

LIDGATE: Pull yourself together, Spence. It's disgraceful to let yourself go like that. Pull yourself together, man! *(He lays a hand on his shoulder and shakes him almost angrily.)*

SPENCE: All right, sir. I'll try.

LIDGATE: In the first place, nothing whatever is going to happen to you. Whatever does happen will happen to me. *I'm* responsible here. And in the second place, even if anything were going to happen to you, it would still be a disgrace to behave as you're doing. If one's a man, it's one's business to behave like a man. Not like a scared animal. Haven't you any pride, man?

SPENCE: *(Making a great effort to recover his self-control.)* I'm sorry, sir. I'm sorry.

LIDGATE: A man's got his human dignity to think of.

SPENCE: Yes, you're quite right, sir. I oughtn't to have let myself go like that. I didn't mean to. But you know how it is: you want to do one thing, and suddenly you find yourself doing just the opposite— you can't help it. It's my nerves, Mr. Lidgate. I haven't been sleeping properly these last weeks.

LIDGATE: Not sleeping? That's bad.

SPENCE: No, sir. I just lie thinking and thinking all night long. And if ever I do drop off, I have such awful dreams—such terrible dreams, Mr. Lidgate, I'm glad to be awake again. It's made me quite ill.

LIDGATE: *(Distressed.)* But why didn't you tell me, Spence? Yes, and why didn't I notice it? Now that you've said it—now that it's too late—I can see you're ill.

SPENCE: But it's nothing really, sir. Just a bit of nerves, that's all. I only wanted to explain—well, you know . . . why I carried on like that just now. Just nerves. It won't happen again, I promise you. I'm ashamed I was so weak. I ask you to excuse me, sir.

LIDGATE: *(Deeply moved, lays his hand on* SPENCE'S *shoulder, then turns away and speaks in a low voice.)* I'm the one to be ashamed, Spence. I'm the one who ought to be asking pardon.

SPENCE: *You* asking pardon of *me*, Mr. Lidgate.

LIDGATE: For dragging you into this—gratuitously, wantonly. I'm sorry, Spence; it was wrong. I begin to realize now how wrong.

SPENCE: But, sir, you had the industry to think of; the interests of the country were at stake. You couldn't allow that Lupton gang to smash up all your work.

LIDGATE: *(Smiling.)* Thank you, Spence. I know you don't mean to be sarcastic.

SPENCE: Sarcastic, Mr. Lidgate? But, I assure you, sir, I never dreamed of such a thing. I was only . . .

LIDGATE: . . . only telling me what I'd told you. I know. But that's where the irony came in.

SPENCE: But you had to try and save the industry, sir. It was your duty; yes, it was your duty, Mr. Lidgate.

LIDGATE: Was it? Well, even if it was, had I any right to sacrifice other people's happiness?

SPENCE: But if other people are glad to be sacrificed, sir . . . if they don't even regard it as a sacrifice . . .

LIDGATE: That only makes my responsibility heavier. But thank you all the same, Spence. *(He shakes Spence by the hand.)* And thank you for everything else. For all the hard work and the patience and the loyalty. And forgive me for everything, Spence. For all the things in the past. And now for getting you into this. But I promise you that you shan't have to suffer, I promise you, Spence.

SPENCE: Oh, sir ... Mr. Lidgate ... *(He looks at* LIDGATE, *speechless with emotion. The telephone bell rings.)*

LIDGATE: Is there never to be any peace? *(He picks up the receiver.)* Hullo ... speaking ... Good evening ... Fire away then ... Oh, is that all! But I knew that long ago ... No, nobody told me. But I knew ... How? Because it was inevitable; it couldn't have been otherwise ... Oh, don't apologize. I don't mind about it, you know ... Yes, I should have minded a few days ago. But not now, not now. What *does* it matter, after all? ... Goodbye, and thank you for ringing up. *(He replaces the receiver and turns back to* SPENCE.) Well, you'll be interested to hear that the Danish contract has gone to Vickers.[52]

SPENCE: For certain, sir?

LIDGATE: Yes, for certain. And what a comfort that is ... being certain. Absolutely certain. And now, Spence, you must go straight home and eat a good dinner and go to bed early and sleep like a log. Like a log, do you hear? And don't bother about anything. Because everything will be perfectly all right as far as you're concerned.

SPENCE: But what about you, sir?

LIDGATE: Perfectly all right as far as I'm concerned too. I'm quite contented. You needn't bother about me. And now go. And don't forget to give my kindest regards to your sister. Tell her I always wear those slippers she embroidered for me. *(During this speech he has been leading* SPENCE *across the room towards the door, which he opens as he pronounces the last sentence.)* Well, good night, Spence.

SPENCE: Good night, Mr. Lidgate. Are you quite sure you don't need me any more?

LIDGATE: No, no. I don't need anything now. Good night. And thank you. Thank you.

SPENCE: Good night, sir. *(He goes out.)*

LIDGATE: *(Shuts the door behind him, then walks back to his table, sits down at it, picks up a sheaf of letters lying in a wicker tray in front of him, then, with a little laugh, tears them across and drops them into the waste paper basket. Then he writes a note, and puts it in an envelope, which he addresses. After that he opens a drawer, takes out a revolver and a box of cartridges, loads the revolver and puts it in his pocket. He gets up, walks to one of the windows, draws the curtain and standing in the deep embrasure behind it, looks out. Beyond the panes is the early darkness of a winter evening. The silhouette of a bare tree lifts its black skeleton against the pinkish gloom of the London night sky.* LIDGATE *whispers to himself.)* "Now more than ever seems it rich to die. Now more than ever . . ." *(He relapses into silence and stands quite still, looking out. The door opens and* BARMBY *comes in; he looks round, does not see* LIDGATE *in the embrasure of the window and walks into the room as if he were alone, whistling softly to himself. He goes to a shelf, takes out a book and is moving towards the fireplace, when he sees* LIDGATE *standing motionless in the window. The shock of surprise makes him start.)*

BARMBY: Goodness! You did give me a start! But what *are* you doing, hiding there, like that?

LIDGATE: *(Stands for a moment longer with his back to* BARMBY, *looking out; then sighs, turns round and comes back into the room.)* I was looking at the night.

BARMBY: Looking at the night? *(He glances out and quickly turns back towards the fire.)* Well, there isn't much to see, is there?

LIDGATE: No, that's the beauty of the night: there's nothing to see. The daylight is full of all kinds of stupid restlessness. But in the night there's nothing. *(They sit down by the fire.)*

BARMBY: I came to see if you felt inclined for what Joan calls "lessons" this evening.

LIDGATE: No, not tonight.

BARMBY: *(Smiling.)* No culture?

LIDGATE: *(Shakes his head. There is a silence.)*

BARMBY: *(Making as if to rise.)* Perhaps you'd like me to go in that case.

LIDGATE: No, please don't. There are some things . . . some things I'd like to say to you, Barmby.

BARMBY: Oh, all right. *(He sits down again.)*

LIDGATE: *(After a pause.)* You'd say I was a successful man, wouldn't you?

BARMBY: Well, you've got what you wanted. Isn't that the definition of success?

LIDGATE: Yes; and then, when one's got it, discovering one didn't really want it at all—that's the result of success.

BARMBY: Still there is always the sport of getting—the fun of doing something skilfully and well. You enjoy that, don't you?

LIDGATE: I did enjoy it. But when one stops to think about it, how hopelessly silly it all seems.

BARMBY: But how hopelessly silly any kind of action is, if you stop to think about it! Moral: don't stop to think.

LIDGATE: You can't help it sometimes.

BARMBY: It's dangerous.

LIDGATE: Why dangerous?

BARMBY: Because all thinking brings you in the long run to the same place. At the end of every corridor you open the same door and find yourself looking over the edge of the same black precipice—down into the darkness of death.

LIDGATE: How did you know it, Barmby?

BARMBY: Know what?

LIDGATE: What was in my mind.

BARMBY: Why, for the simple reason that, if you start thinking at all, you must think about death. Finally and ultimately, there's nothing else to think about. At the end of every corridor, I tell you. And when one looks into the black hole, everything else seems silly. Not only your absurd finance but my ridiculous literature and Walter Clough's idiotic communism. Yes, and even Shakespeare's poetry and Newton's science and St. Francis's religion—all utterly and hopelessly silly, so far as the individual is concerned. Because, whatever he may be or do or think or feel, the individual is mortal. Condemned to death. He goes whizzing along his little rails. Full speed ahead, all clear on the line. And then suddenly the rails break off and over he goes, into the black hole. And where there was something, suddenly there isn't anything. Finished.

LIDGATE: Are you afraid of death, Barmby?

BARMBY: Terrified, when I think of it. That's why I do my best not to think of it.

LIDGATE: And yet the comfort of death, Barmby! The simplicity, "Now more than ever seems it rich to die." Rich! Too rich, in a way. It seems rather selfish somehow—do you see what I mean? Selfish to be so supremely well off, when other people have to go on in their misery. It's the one thing that makes me doubt—makes me wonder whether one has the right to . . . Oh! *(It is* JOAN *who, having entered very quietly, still in her outdoor clothes, lays a hand on his shoulder.* LIDGATE *looks up, startled, sees her, and a distressed, almost guilty look appears on his face.)* Oh, it's you, Joan.

JOAN: Yes, it's me. *(She sighs.)* And I wish it wasn't. *(She sits down and pulls off her hat.)* Why does one always have to be oneself?

BARMBY: *(Speaking with a trace of mockery.)* You've been a long time getting back from Walter's.

JOAN: *(Wearily.)* Yes, I walked most of the way. *(Suddenly looking up at him and in a sharper questioning voice.)* But how did you know I'd been at Walter's?

BARMBY: Because I went there to meet you. As you asked me to. At six o'clock precisely.

JOAN: Oh, of course, I'd forgotten.

BARMBY: I know you had. And next time you make me traipse up to Camden Town,[53] I'll trouble you not to forget.

JOAN: *(With a sudden malignant little laugh.)* It served you right.

BARMBY: Served me right? What for?

JOAN: For everything. For being you. Always and hopelessly and inevitably you. *(In a changed voice, dully and miserably.)* And anyhow, it won't ever happen again. Never. *(She turns to* LIDGATE.*)* Oh, Daddy, why did you want to go and make all this idiotic money? What's the

BARMBY: No, I suppose one can't really hesitate.

LIDGATE: *(After a pause.)* And then there's Joan to think of. The trial, all the obscene publicity—I want to spare her *that* humiliation. And then God knows what I might become in prison. A sort of half-mad, cringing animal. A lot of them go that way. And that would be her father. No; better end it at once, cleanly. It'll be horrible for her. Horrible. But less horrible than the other thing. Don't you think so?

BARMBY: *(After a pause, and in a low voice.)* Yes.

LIDGATE: You'll try . . . You'll try to help her a bit, won't you?

BARMBY: I'll do my best.

LIDGATE: Try to explain to her a bit, later on. Why I did it.

BARMBY: Very well.

LIDGATE: And ask her to forgive me—forgive me for not having loved her more. For having loved her too much in a way, as well. Perhaps if her mother had lived . . . *(There is a silence. Then taking a deep breath, he turns to* BARMBY.*)* I think you'd better go now, Barmby.

BARMBY: *(Gets up.)*

LIDGATE: There's a letter on the table there. But they'll find it all right. I wanted to make it quite clear that poor old Spence had nothing to do with the business. Well, goodbye, Barmby.

BARMBY: Goodbye. *(They shake hands.* BARMBY *goes out.* LIDGATE *stands for some time leaning against the mantelpiece. Then crosses the room and turns out the lights. Seen only by the glow of the fire, he walks back, across the stage and comes to a standstill by the writing table. He takes the revolver out of his pocket. The* CURTAIN *slowly descends.)*

Epilogue

*(The same, four days later). It is morning; a London garden bounded by walls and chimney pots, is visible through the window. *JOAN* is sitting at the table writing. She is dressed in her outdoor clothes and wears a hat. *BARMBY* is standing beside her.)*

JOAN: *(Laying down the pen, and handing *BARMBY* the sheet of paper on which she has been writing.)* There. That's my address. If there's anything urgent, you can write or telegraph there.

BARMBY: *(After looking at the paper, folds it and puts it away in his pocket book.)* I see.

JOAN: But don't tell anyone where I am. Do you understand, Phil? Nobody whatever. Can I rely on you for that?

BARMBY: Yes, you can rely on me.

JOAN: And don't forward any letters. I don't even want to hear from anybody. *(Leaning wearily back in her chair.)* Oh, dear, how awful it is that everything goes on—goes on and on, just the same as ever! The buses and the theatres and the tea shops and all the people in the streets, and Upavon's beastly papers every morning and evening. On and on and on.

BARMBY: But, isn't it really a consolation? Life persisting and renewing itself. Even Upavon's papers are good, when you think of them in that light.

JOAN: Yes, I suppose so. But all the same it upsets me; it makes me feel uncomfortable and . . . and somehow ashamed. Ashamed of still being hungry and eating my three meals a day as though nothing had happened; and being sleepy and going to bed at night and waking up again next morning—waking up and then suddenly remembering that there's someone who won't ever wake up again. *(A silence. She looks at her watch.)* Well, I must be thinking of going. *(She gets up.)* You've been very sweet, Phil. You're a nice man, you know; a very decent man really.

BARMBY: *(Shakes his head.)* No, I'm not.

JOAN: Yes, you are. Only sometimes you don't give yourself a chance of being decent. I shan't forget what you've done for me. *(BARMBY takes her hand and kisses it. She turns away and picks up her bag and walks towards the door; at the door she turns back again.)* If you see Walter, tell him . . . *(She hesitates for a long time.)* Tell him . . .

BARMBY: Tell him what?

JOAN: Oh, I don't know! *(She makes a hopeless gesture. Her voice breaks: she turns away her face; as she goes out, UPAVON comes into the room.)*

UPAVON: Joan! Are you . . . ?

JOAN: *(Sobbing.)* No, no, I can't stay. *(She hurries out.)*

UPAVON: Poor girl! I wish there was something one could do for her.

BARMBY: One can leave her alone. It's easy; and it's the only thing that she wants or that will do her any good.

UPAVON: Yes, I expect you're right. Hasn't Ted Monmouth turned up yet?

BARMBY: Not so far as I'm aware.

UPAVON: *(Looking at his watch.)* I shan't have the right to start cursing for another four minutes. *(Looks round.)* Poor old Arthur! When one thinks what he must have gone through. In this very room.

BARMBY: Yes, what he must have gone through! People who victimize themselves for an idea—I've never been able to understand them. Particularly when it's a thoroughly bad idea. Sacrificing yourself for the greater glory of God—that's just comprehensible. But sacrificing yourself for the greater glory of the iron and steel industry—no, that's utterly beyond me.

UPAVON: *(After a pause.)* What do you think of doing, now, Barmby?

BARMBY: Doing. Oh, the usual thing. Nothing in particular.

UPAVON: I've got a job for you.

BARMBY: A job? Heaven preserve us!

UPAVON: What do you say to the literary editorship of the *Daily Gazette?*

BARMBY: *Literary* editorship of the *Gazette?* Isn't it a contradiction in terms?

UPAVON: The present man's going. I need someone to take his place. Will you do it, Barmby?

BARMBY: No, I won't.

UPAVON: But you don't realize. It's a good job. We pay very well on the *Gazette.*

BARMBY: I know. But after all one's got to draw the line somewhere. Besides, I could never get down to the office in the mornings.[55]
(A FOOTMAN *appears at the door.)*

FOOTMAN: There's a gentleman would like to see you, sir.

BARMBY: Who? Me?

FOOTMAN: Yes, sir.

CLOUGH: *(Coming into the room.)* It's only me, Phil. Can you spare me half a minute? I'm sorry to interrupt you. But it's rather urgent.
(The FOOTMAN *goes out.)*

BARMBY: *(Gets up and goes to meet him. They talk standing near the door.)* What is it, Walter?

CLOUGH: I was away, when this thing happened—had to be in Barcelona for a conference, and only got back this morning. Otherwise I'd have come before. Tell me, how's Joan? It must have been too awful for her.

BARMBY: It was—horrible.

CLOUGH: Where is she? I want to see her.

BARMBY: You can't. She's gone—not five minutes ago.

CLOUGH: Where to?

BARMBY: Into the country.

CLOUGH: But where?

BARMBY: I can't tell you. She made me promise I wouldn't give her address—not to anyone.

CLOUGH: Don't be a fool! I'm not anyone. You know that quite well. Tell me where.

BARMBY: Shall I? *(Hesitates.)* All right, I'll take the risk of disobeying her. *(He looks at his watch.)* If you jump into a taxi and drive straight to Paddington, you'll be in time to catch her. She's travelling by the twelve o'clock train to Exeter.[56] *(MONMOUTH enters the room, while he is saying this.)* You've got eighteen minutes.

CLOUGH: Eighteen minutes. That's plenty. *(He turns to go and finds himself face to face with MONMOUTH.)*

MONMOUTH: Ah, we meet again.

CLOUGH: *(Ferociously.)* Oh, damn your eyes! *(He rushes out.)*

MONMOUTH: What is the matter with the chap? Has he gone mad?

BARMBY: *(Taking his arm and leading him across the room to where* UPAVON *is sitting.)* Just a touch of temporary insanity, that's all.

UPAVON: *(Watch in hand, severely.)* Two minutes late, Ted.

MONMOUTH: I'm so sorry. You see, my taxi . . .

UPAVON: I know, I know. You had a puncture in Piccadilly.[57] One day I shall get annoyed and give you the sack. So choose your taxis more carefully in future. *(In another tone.)* Well, I've made up my mind about the house. I'll take over the rest of poor Arthur's lease. On the same terms.

MONMOUTH: Oh, that's splendid!

UPAVON: Occupation begins from tomorrow.

MONMOUTH: From today if you like.

UPAVON: All right, from today. From this moment. You're *my* guest now. I'll sign the papers as soon as your lawyer can draw them up.

MONMOUTH: I'll see that they're ready tomorrow.

UPAVON: Whenever you like.

MONMOUTH: Well, that *is* a load off my mind. Having the house thrown back on my hands like this—I can't tell you what a worry that was. And not the smallest prospect of getting anything out of Lidgate's estate for the rest of the lease. My word, I should have been in a hole! But you've saved the situation. I'm eternally grateful to you.

UPAVON: Oh, don't bother about eternity, Ted. Two or three weeks will be quite sufficient. Listen, Ted, I want you to go easy for a bit on the gossip.

MONMOUTH: How do you mean?

UPAVON: I'm launching our great public economy campaign tomorrow.

BARMBY: *(Under his breath.)* Oh, Lord!

UPAVON: We shall be calling for retrenchment on unemployment and education—all the social services, in fact. Sacrifices all round. And one of the sacrifices will have to be you. All that stuff of yours about fancy dress parties at the Embassy and Mr. Goldberg's ivory and ebony bedroom—it's first-rate, absolutely first-rate. But not while we're running the economy campaign.

MONMOUTH: Yes, I can see that.

UPAVON: It's out of the picture. It's irrelevant. Now listen, Ted: during the economy campaign, no parties. That's the first thing.

MONMOUTH: I'd better make a note of it. *(He takes out a small notebook and pencil.)* "No parties."

UPAVON: I don't mind a debutante's coming-out dance: that's the family; that's respectable. And of course, anything that's for charity. You mustn't miss anything charitable, do you understand?

MONMOUTH: *(He writes.)* "Except debs and charity."

UPAVON: Don't meet your friends at the Embassy. Meet them at bazaars.

MONMOUTH: *(Writing.)* "Bazaars." I see.

UPAVON: And then go down into the country and stay with people who farm their estates. That's always good. "The Countess super-intending work on her model farm." You'd better take a photographer along with you.

MONMOUTH: Right you are.

UPAVON: And talk a bit about the older people for a change. Old respectable people. I suppose you still know a few of those. I want the tone of the gossip column to be extremely high while we're running economy. High and pure.

MONMOUTH: *(Writing.)* "High and pure."

UPAVON: After the campaign's over, you can do what you like. But for the next three weeks, mind! *(He shakes his finger at MONMOUTH.)*

(FOOTMAN opens the door and announces, "Miss Endicott." Enter PEGGY.)

PEGGY: *(As they rise.)* No, don't get up; please don't get up. How are you, Lord Upavon? And Phil! *(She waves her hand to him across the table.)* Ted darling! *(She sits down.)* Do you know I haven't been here since . . . since it happened. It was actually in this room, wasn't it?

UPAVON: Yes, in this room.

PEGGY: Too awful! Has anyone seen Joan these last days?

BARMBY: She's gone down to the country. To hide. She doesn't want to see anyone.

PEGGY: Poor Joan! She *was* such a charming girl!

BARMBY: Why speak of her as though she were dead? She still is a charming girl.

PEGGY: *(Slightly confused.)* Oh, of course, of course. But somehow one feels . . . one feels that she's gone out of one's life. Don't you feel that, Ted?

MONMOUTH: Yes, yes. I know just what you mean.

BARMBY: I wish I did. You mean you don't think you'll go on being friendly with her because she's lost all her money—is that it?

PEGGY: No, no. Of *course* not. What has that got to do with it?

BARMBY: I should have thought it had a great deal to do with it.

PEGGY: No, it's something *quite* different. Isn't it, Ted?

MONMOUTH: Absolutely different.

PEGGY: Something—how shall I put it? Something almost *mystical*.

BARMBY: Crikey!

PEGGY: As though a whole *chapter* of one's life had come to an end with that pistol shot. *(She nods slowly and sighs.)* Ted, are you coming to help me choose my skiing clothes for St. Moritz?[58]

MONMOUTH: Yes, what fun! I saw the most ravishing sweaters in Fortnum's window yesterday.[59] Longed to get one for myself.

PEGGY: Come on, then. Well, goodbye, Lord Upavon. Goodbye, Phil.

MONMOUTH: *(To* UPAVON.*)* I'll let you know when the papers are ready for signing.

UPAVON: All right. And don't forget what I told you about the gossip.

MONMOUTH: No, no. "High and pure, High and pure." Come on, Peggy. *(He lays a hand familiarly on her shoulder, and they go out in a walking embrace.)*

UPAVON: I hear they're going to get married, those two.

BARMBY: Her father's rich, isn't he?

UPAVON: Yes; frozen meat.

BARMBY: Frozen meat? *(He nods slowly.* CURTAIN.*)*

Notes

Introduction

1. *Letters of Aldous Huxley*, ed. Grover Smith (London: Chatto and Windus, 1969), 157. Hereafter, *Letters*.

2. *Letters*, 187.

3. *Letters*, 964. By "over here," Huxley meant California, where he had lived since 1937.

4. "This play," Sybille Bedford writes of *Now More Than Ever*, "was never produced, or published, and the typescript appears lost," *Aldous Huxley: A Biography* (London: Chatto and Windus in association with Collins, 1973), 1:257. Three years later, however, Pierre Vitoux pinpointed the "most important" single item in the Harry Ransom Humanities Research Center's (HRHRC's) Huxley Collection as being "the complete typescript of Huxley's play *Now More Than Ever*," "Aldous Huxley at Texas: A Checklist of Manuscripts," *Library Chronicle of the University of Texas at Austin* 9 (1976): 41–58.

5. "Interviews with Great Scientists (VII): Aldous Huxley," *Observer* (1 February 1931): 15–16. Reprinted as "Mr. Aldous Huxley," in J. W. N. Sullivan, *Contemporary Mind: Some Modern Answers* (London: Humphrey Toulmin, 1934), 141–147.

6. For Huxley's firsthand response to the social effects of the Slump in England, see Aldous Huxley, *Between the Wars: Essays and Letters*, ed. David Bradshaw (Chicago: Ivan R. Dee, 1994) (hereafter *BW*), xii–xxvi, 51–95, and David Bradshaw, "Huxley's Slump," in *The Art of Literary Biography*, ed. John Batchelor (Oxford: Clarendon Press, 1995), 151–171.

7. See David Bradshaw, "The Flight from Gaza: Aldous Huxley's Involvement with the Peace Pledge Union in the Context of His Overall Intellectual Development," *"Now More Than Ever": Proceedings of the Aldous Huxley Centenary Symposium Münster 1994* (Frankfurt am Main and New York: Peter Lang, 1995), 9–27. Quote from p. 11.

8. Aldous Huxley, preface to *This Way to Paradise*, by Campbell Dixon (London: Chatto and Windus, 1930), n. page. See also *Letters*, 327–329. The play ran from 30 January to 1 March 1930 at Daly's Theatre in London.

9. These plays are *Red and White*, *Letters*, 183, which is now lost; *Permutations Among the Nightingales*, *Coterie* (Easter 1920), 68–93; and *Happy Families*, *Limbo* (London: Chatto and Windus, 1920), 211–244.

10. "Albert: Prince Consort," *Vanity Fair* 18 (March 1922): 33–34, 98; and "The Ambassador of Capripedia," *Vanity Fair* 18 (May 1922): 61, 112.

11. "A Film with a Warning," *Vanity Fair* 19 (October 1922): 59, 98; "The Publisher—A Comedy in Five Scenes," *Vanity Fair* 20 (April 1923): 53, 116; and "A Marriage of Inconvenience," *Vanity Fair* 21 (September 1923): 38, 90.

12. Huxley to Mary Hutchinson, HRHRC, 16 January 1923. As Alec Waugh was first to note, the Cave of Harmony is the original of the nightclub in chapters 15 and 16 of *Antic Hay* (1923). See *The Early Years of Alec Waugh* (London: Cassell, 1962), 184.

13. Nigel Playfair, *Hammersmith Hoy: A Book of Minor Revelations* (London: Faber and Faber, 1930), 251.

14. Aldous Huxley, *The World of Light: A Comedy in Three Acts* (London: Chatto and Windus, 1931), 11.

15. Desmond MacCarthy, "Mr. Aldous Huxley, The Stage and the Spirits," *New Statesman and Nation* 1 (11 April 1931): 251–252.

16. Leon M. Lion, *The Surprise of My Life: The Lesser Half of an Autobiography* (London: Hutchinson, 1948), 14.

17. Huxley to J. Ralph Pinker, HRHRC, 24 July 1932. Partly quoted in *Letters*, 364. J. Ralph Pinker ran the London office of the J. B. Pinker literary agency.

18. Allen Churchill, *The Incredible Ivar Kreuger* (London: Weidenfeld and Nicolson, 1957), 15. For other discussions of Kreuger, see Trevor Allen, *Ivar Kreuger: Match King, Croesus, and Crook* (London: John Long, 1932); Manfred Georg, *The Case of Ivar Kreuger: An Adventure in Finance*, trans. L. M. Sieveking and Ian F. D. Morrow (London: Jonathan Cape, 1933); Robert Shaplen, *Kreuger, Genius and Swindler* (London: Andre Deutsch, 1961); and George Soloveytchik, *The Financier: The Life of Ivar Kreuger* (London: Peter Davies, 1933).

19. Richard Aldington, review of Evelyn Waugh's *Vile Bodies*, *Sunday Referee* (9 February 1930): 6. Quoted in Martin Stannard, *Evelyn Waugh: The Critical Heritage* (London: Routledge and Kegan Paul, 1984), 102–105. Quote from pp. 103–104.

20. "Kreuger lying shot in the Paris Hotel was his example," Graham Greene, *England Made Me* (London: Heinemann, 1935), 46.

21. Graham Greene, *Ways of Escape* (London: Bodley Head, 1980), 46.

22. Lion, *The Surprise of My Life*, 115.

23. Quoted in Soloveytchik, *The Financier*, 174–175.

24. Both Poincaré and Keynes are quoted in Torsten Kreuger, *The Truth About Ivar Kreuger: Eye-Witness Accounts, Secret Files, Documents* (Stuttgart: Seewald Verlag, 1968), 69.

25. *Letters*, 363.

26. Huxley to J. Ralph Pinker, HRHRC, 10 October 1932.

27. *Letters*, 364.

28. Clementine Robert, *Aldous Huxley, Exhumations: Correspondance inédite avec Sydney Schiff (1925–1937)* (Paris: Didier, 1976), 75.

29. Derek Patmore, "Writers of To-Day. No. 2: Aldous Huxley," *Sunday Referee* (25 December 1932): 6.

30. Huxley had followed Hatry's trial at the beginning of 1930 (*Letters*, 327). On 26 January 1930, Hatry was found guilty of what the judge at his trial called "the most appalling fraud that ever disfigured the commercial reputation of this City." Hatry received a prison sentence of fourteen years for issuing forged securities for the cities of Wakefield, Newcastle, and Liverpool. The character of the eponymous Chawdron, a speculator and "large scale, Napoleonic crook," is obviously based

on Hatry, Aldous Huxley, "Chawdron," *Life and Letters* 4 (April 1930): 255-302. Reprinted in *Brief Candles* (1930).

31. *BW,* 116.

32. Lion, *The Surprise of My Life,* 113.

33. Ashley Dukes, "The London Scene," *Theatre Arts* 15 (June 1931): 459-460. Produced in 1892, *Widowers' Houses* was George Bernard Shaw's first play.

34. Aldous Huxley, review of *Plays: Fourth Series,* by John Galsworthy, *Athenaeum* (4 June 1920): 733.

35. Aldous Huxley, review of *The Melting Pot,* by Israel Zangwill, *Westminster Gazette* (9 December 1920): 6.

36. *Letters,* 560 note.

37. Huxley to J. Ralph Pinker, HRHRC, 25 May 1933.

38. Huxley to J. Ralph Pinker, HRHRC, 11 June 1933.

39. Huxley to J. Ralph Pinker, HRHRC, 22 June 1934.

40. Huxley to J. Ralph Pinker, HRHRC, 18 December 1934. For an account of the Shilling Theatre, see Norman Marshall, *The Other Theatre* (London: John Lehmann, 1947), 218.

41. Robert Medley to David Bradshaw, 16 September 1984. In the possession of David Bradshaw.

42. Michael J. Sidnell, *Dances of Death: The Group Theatre of London in the Thirties* (London: Faber and Faber, 1984), 258.

43. *BW,* 63.

44. *BW,* xvii; see also *Aldous Huxley's Hearst Essays,* ed. James Sexton (New York and London: Garland, 1994), 116 (hereafter *HE).*

45. Julian Huxley, *If I Were Dictator* (London: Methuen, 1934), 16.

46. L. Urwick, *The Meaning of Rationalisation* (London: Nisbet, 1929), v.

47. Sir Mark Webster Jenkinson, *Some Aspects of Rationalization* (London: Gee, 1929), 5.

48. *BW,* 67-68. See also James Sexton, *"Brave New World* and the Rationalization of Industry," *English Studies in Canada* 12 (1986): 424-436, reprinted in *Critical Essays on Aldous Huxley,* ed. Jerome Meckier (New York: G. K. Hall, 1996), 88-102.

49. Aldous Huxley, *Jesting Pilate* (London: Chatto and Windus, 1926), 99.

50. *HE,* 222.

51. Vilfredo Pareto, *The Mind and Society,* trans. Andrew Bongiorno and Arthur Livingston, 4 vols. (London: Jonathan Cape, 1935), iv, 1646.

52. Aldous Huxley, *Point Counter Point* (London: Chatto and Windus, 1928), 416.

53. *Letters,* 341. See also Bradshaw, "Huxley's Slump."

54. *BW,* 79-80. For further details of Huxley's Wellsian interest in a global panacea to the world's economic problems, see *BW,* 36-37 .

55. Aldous Huxley, *Brave New World* (London: Chatto and Windus, 1932), 34, 278.

56. As Malthus put it in his *Principles of Political Economy,* "if production be in a great excess above consumption, the motive to accumulate and produce must cease

from the want of a will to consume," T. R. Malthus, *Principles of Political Economy Considered with a View to Their Practical Application* (London: John Murray, 1820), 9.

57. Keynes accepted overproduction as a basic feature of capitalism and championed Malthus in his account of the earlier controversy. See J. M. Keynes, *Essays in Biography* (London: Macmillan, 1933), 144. See also Keynes's *The General Theory of Employment, Interest and Money* (London: Macmillan, 1936), 362–371.

58. A. J. P. Taylor, *English History 1914-1945* (London: Oxford University Press, 1965), 339. Clay wrote, "The recurrence of over-production . . . is connected with the fundamental principle of the present system, specialisation, with its outcome, production in anticipation of demand . . . The loss and suffering caused by trade fluctuations are largely concentrated on the poor, and the sense of helplessness which unemployment brings to a man is an affliction of the spirit even heavier than the material loss that accompanies it," Clay, *Economics,* 257.

59. *Letters,* 359–360.

60. *Letters,* 370.

Play Text

1. Berkeley Square is located in an exclusive district of London immediately north of Piccadilly. Its former residents include the politicians William Pitt the Elder, Charles James Fox, and George Canning. Huxley's imaginary Monmouth House is partly modeled on Devonshire House, Piccadilly, London home of the Dukes of Devonshire, built in 1734-1737 and demolished in 1924. Built in the 1680s and demolished in 1773, the real Monmouth House, in Soho Square, was briefly the home of James Scott, Duke of Monmouth and illegitimate son of Charles II. He was executed in 1685 after his unsuccessful rebellion.

2. Thomas Lupton was the author of *A Moral and Pitieful Comedie, Intituled, All for Money. Plainly representing the manners of men, and fashson of the world noweadayes* (1578). Huxley seems also to have had in mind Sir Thomas Lipton (1850-1931), who rose from humble Glaswegian origins to become a millionaire by the age of thirty. At the time of his death, Lipton had become one of the most successful entrepreneurs of his era.

3. Jehoshaphat was a king of Judah (2 *Samuel* 8:16, etc.); his name had been used in interjections expressing surprise, excitement, or alarm (as in "jumping Jehoshaphat!") since the mid-nineteenth century.

4. Probably an allusion to John Collier's racy and much discussed novel, *His Monkey Wife: Or, Married to a Chimp* (London: P. Davies, 1930), which tells the story of an English schoolmaster who marries a prodigious chimpanzee named Emily.

5. Upper Brook Street extends from Grosvenor Square to Park Lane through London's Mayfair district. The street remained almost entirely residential until 1939 and was particularly favored by the aristocracy, the very wealthy, and the governing elite.

6. This character is based on the Canadian newspaper proprietor William Maxwell Aitken (1879–1964), first Baron Beaverbrook. Having emigrated to Britain in 1910, he purchased the *Daily Express* in 1916. Through it and other newspapers in his stable, Beaverbrook campaigned with untiring zeal for what he called "Empire Free Trade." "One of the talents Max Aitken exhibited throughout his long life lay in confecting combines and alliances. In 1909 he formed the Canada Cement Company, a controversial amalgamation much criticized in some quarters, the echoes of which, much to his righteous indignation, were to reverberate about his ears for years to come," *Dictionary of National Biography*.

7. The American businessman Frank Winfield Woolworth (1852–1919) opened his first "walk around shopping" store in Britain in 1909 and others soon followed. In each branch, the price of all goods was one penny, three pennies, or sixpence, and, as a result, the name Woolworth soon became synonymous (in Britain, at least) with cheapness. London's first Woolworth's store opened in 1916.

8. Although Lidgate's surname links him with the English medieval poet John Lydgate (?1370–ca. 1450), whose last and longest work was *The Falle of Princis*, written between 1431 and 1438, Lidgate is based on the Swedish financier and fraudster Ivar Kreuger (1880–1932); see Introduction. In "Proletarian Literature," Huxley wrote: "The protagonists of all the ancient epics and dramas were invariably kings and queens, princes and princesses, the great ones of the earth . . . Imaginative literature still deals with the great ones of the earth, but the great ones are no longer nobles. They are financiers, manufacturers, professional men," *HE*, 209.

9. Along with Thomas Gainsborough and Joshua Reynolds, George Romney was one of the most famous English portrait painters of the late eighteenth century.

10. George Hepplewhite (d. 1786) was a British craftsman whose London furniture workshop was particularly famous for its simple and elegant style of chairs. He worked mainly in mahogany and satinwood.

11. The economic slump which followed the 1929 Wall Street Crash gave impetus to the growing vogue for industrial rationalization; see Introduction. The adage "First catch your hare" is generally attributed to Hannah Glasse, habit-maker to the Prince of Wales and the author of *The Art of Cookery, Made Plain and Easy, by a Lady* (1747, etc.). Lupton, of course, plays on other meanings of the verb "to cook": to concoct, make up, invent, or falsify.

12. As his article entitled "Abroad in England" (1931) makes plain, Huxley was drawn to Middlesbrough, in the northeast of England, because of its status as "a characteristic product of nineteenth-century civilization." As such, it suffered badly when the economic slump took hold. "Ugly and dismal enough even in its best days," Huxley wrote, "it is now, in the hour of its misfortune, unspeakably gloomy, a sort of city of the dead," *BW*, 59–60; see also 61 and 65.

13. Portsmouth is a city and major naval port lying on the Hampshire coast seventy-four miles southwest of London. In the early 1930s, Coventry, in the English west Midlands, was primarily an industrial city. Nottingham, a city in the east Midlands, was mainly dependent upon engineering, coal mining, pharmaceuticals, lace, and textiles in the 1930s. In 1929, the swindler Clarence Hatry illegally inflated the values of municipal bonds for Swindon (an important railway center

in Wiltshire, seventy-seven miles west of London), Gloucester (a city in the west of England), and Wakefield (a city in the northern county of Yorkshire), precipitating a major financial crisis in the City of London; see Introduction.

14. The brunt of the world depression in cotton between the wars was centered on Lancashire, a county in the northwest of England. Like Lidgate, Huxley was a zealous advocate of planning; see *BW*, xvii–xviii, xx, xxii, 62–64, 66–67, 86, 210–214, 220. Huxley may have had in mind Henry Clay's *Report on the Position of the English Cotton Industry* (London: Nisbet, 1931) at this point in the play.

15. To some extent a Huxleyan self-portrait, Barmby has much in common with Philip Quarles in *Point Counter Point* (1928), Anthony Beavis in *Eyeless in Gaza* (1936), and Jeremy Pordage in *After Many a Summer: A Novel* (1939). When naming this character, Huxley may have had in mind Arthur William Barmby, who had been in charge of his friend D. H. Lawrence's affairs at the Curtis Brown literary agency in New York—Huxley's edition of Lawrence's *Letters* was published in September 1932—but the character clearly owes much more to John Goodwyn Barmby (1820–1881), the Christian socialist who claimed to have invented the term "communism" while on a visit to Paris in 1840. In 1841, Barmby founded the Communist Propaganda Society.

16. Agricultural overproduction greatly concerned Huxley at this time; see, for instance, *BW*, 80–81.

17. Like many of his contemporaries, Huxley wrote fulsomely in praise of the Soviet Union in the early 1930s. See Bradshaw, "Huxley's Slump," and *BW*, xviii–xix and 62–63.

18. A thinly veiled reference to Beaverbrook's press crusade for "Empire Free Trade," the system of tariff concessions granted by members of the British Empire to one another, otherwise known as imperial preference. See chapters 11–13 of A. J. P. Taylor, *Beaverbrook* (London: Hamish Hamilton, 1972), 246–326, esp. chapter 12, "The Crusader, 1930–31," 272–307.

19. The ensuing discussion of economics owes a great deal to Huxley's reading of Fred Henderson's *The Economic Consequences of Power Production* (London: Allen and Unwin, 1931) and George Bernard Shaw's *The Intelligent Woman's Guide to Socialism and Capitalism* (London: Constable, 1928); see Introduction and Huxley's "Compulsory Suicide," *HE*, 107.

20. Transatlantic telegraph cables had been in service since 1866, but owing to bandwidth limitations these cables could not be used for voice transmission. However, a regular transatlantic telephone service between the United States and Europe via radio was first established in 1927.

21. In "Science and Civilisation" (1932), Huxley observed, "The abstruse researches of Faraday and Clerk Maxwell have resulted, among other things, in the jazz band at the Savoy Hotel being audible in Timbuctoo," *BW*, 113.

22. Brondesbury is a district of northwest London. The reasons for " 'England Changing Hands' " in this way are examined by Peter Mandler, *The Fall and Rise of the Stately Home* (New Haven and London: Yale University Press, 1997), esp. part 3, "White Elephants, 1914–1939," 223–263. Quote from p. 228.

23. "Chippendale" refers to Thomas Chippendale (ca. 1718–1779), an English

cabinetmaker who worked mainly in dark mahogany; "Jacobean" is a term applied to the very different style of architecture and furniture in vogue during the reign of James I (1603-1625).

24. The *Daily Sketch* (1908-1971) was purchased by Beaverbrook in 1923. He subsequently passed it on to Harold Sidney Harmsworth, first Viscount Rothermere (1868-1940), and in 1928 it was acquired by Allied Newspapers.

25. *Psalm 42: 7:* "Deep calleth unto deep at the noise of thy waterspouts: all thy waves and thy billows are gone over me."

26. In 1930, when the proprietor of the *Saturday Review* pledged its support for Beaverbrook's "Empire Free Trade" campaign, the magazine's "young and talented Editor, Gerald Barry, thereupon resigned, with almost all his editorial team . . . In a miraculously short time, with new backing, they brought out a new and brighter *Week-End Review,* produced by a lively band of new contributors who set themselves to exposing the "Old Gang" and their out-of-date, ineffectual ways of running the country," Max Nicholson, "Prologue: The Proposal for a National Plan," in *Fifty Years of Political and Economic Planning: Looking Forward 1931-1981,* ed. John Pinder (London: Heinemann, 1981), 5-8. Quote from p. 6. The *Week-End Review* was absorbed by the *New Statesman and Nation* in 1934. It was Max Nicholson who wrote the *Week-End Review*'s "National Plan For Great Britain," a sixteen-page supplement to the 14 February 1931 issue of the magazine. Huxley described this plan as a "rather more fully worked-out plan" than that put forward by Sir Oswald Mosley around about the same time, *BW, 63*; see also note 44. Huxley was a contributor to the *Week-End Review.*

27. For a firsthand account of "the increased appetite of the public for every form of gossip" in the 1930s, and especially titbits about the upper crust, see Patrick Balfour, *Society Racket: A Critical Survey of Modern Social Life* (London: John Long, 1933), 84-105. Quote from p. 84. Balfour also discusses the inter-war legislation and financial pressures which forced members of the aristocracy, such as himself, to make a living by feeding this appetite.

28. In his 1946 foreword to *Brave New World,* reprinted with every subsequent edition, Huxley looked back to the time he wrote his novel in 1931 and described his former self as "an amused, Pyrrhonic aesthete."

29. Ever since merchants from the Lombardy region of north central Italy settled in and around this thoroughfare of the City of London in the twelfth century, Lombard Street has been a synecdoche for London's banking world.

30. The London Hippodrome, on Cranbourn Street, central London, was a very popular music hall theatre which opened in 1900. Between the wars it was famous for its musical comedies. Reconstructed in 1958, it closed in 1991.

31. Chelsea is a district of west London, north of the Thames, where many artists lived and worked. Given its reputation for loose, bohemian living, Peggy is surprised that she has encountered so many "complications" there.

32. Huxley made two visits to Hyde Park, London, in the early 1930s which he described and discussed in subsequent essays. He draws on both pieces in this scene; see "Hyde Park on Sunday," *HE,* 35-36, and "Notes on the Way," *Time and Tide* 13 (7 May 1932): 514-516. On both occasions, Huxley was struck by the

docility of the crowds he encountered at Speakers' Corner (located at the northeast corner of Hyde Park, adjacent to Marble Arch, and still a forum for oratory today) and their amiable toleration of the fervid rhetoric directed at them each and every Sunday of the year. In the *Time and Tide* essay, Huxley wrote: "I was in Hyde Park last autumn on the anniversary of the October Revolution, and again this First of May. I left on both occasions feeling glad I wasn't a Communist speaker. Against the gentle and humorous indifference of the London crowd the fiercest enthusiasm seems to hurl itself in vain . . ."

33. Huxley seems to have drawn on at least two originals for Walter Clough. One was "the Communist orator" he listened to with sympathy in Hyde Park in October 1931 and whom he describes in "Hyde Park on Sunday" (see note 32). The other (possibly the same man) was the "young Jewish . . . communist" who took Huxley to a Jewish abattoir in the East End of London in February 1931, *BW*, 94. There is also a great deal of the early 1930s Huxley himself in Clough, including his Oxford education, though not his membership of the Communist Party of Great Britain. Huxley may have borrowed Clough's name from Arthur Hugh Clough (1819–1861), doubting poet and close friend of his great-uncle, Matthew Arnold.

34. The first verse of a hymn by J. M. Neale (1818–1866).

35. A district of London, south of the Thames, situated between Rotherhithe in the north and Forest Hill in the south. It acquired a reputation as a center of nonconformism in the seventeenth century. Later on, John Wesley was a frequent visitor to and preacher in Peckham.

36. St. James's Park is the oldest of London's Royal Parks and covers about ninety acres of central London. Horse Guards, in Whitehall, was constructed in 1750–1758 after a design by William Kent. Two mounted troopers of the Household Cavalry (comprising The Life Guards and The Blues and Royals) are posted outside Horse Guards each day from 10:00 A.M. to 4:00 P.M. and are relieved every hour.

37. An allusion to Oliver Goldsmith's "The Deserted Village: A Poem" (1770): "And fools, who came to scoff, remained to pray" (l.180).

38. First verse of a hymn by Charles Wesley (1707–1788).

39. "La bêtise n'est pas mon fort" (Stupidity isn't my strong point) are the opening words of *La Soirée avec Monsieur Teste* (1896) by Paul Valéry (1871–1945). Huxley quotes Monsieur Teste's phrase in *Beyond the Mexique Bay* (1934) and again in *The Devils of Loudun* (1952).

40. An imaginary daily newspaper. Between 1908–1926 there had been a *Daily Gazette* published locally in the London borough of Islington.

41. Huxley seems to have had in mind a party attended by his friend Raymond Mortimer in November 1931. According to Michael De-la-Noy, Mortimer "reported [to Edward Sackville-West] (in a letter full of typically uncouth social references of the time) on 'a young Jew' called Jeffres, who had taken 'a vast dismantled house in Regent's Park' in order to throw a party for which he had engaged 'an excellent nigger band.' Apparently everyone had been obliged to wear red and white"; see Michael De-la-Noy, *Eddy: The Life of Edward Sackville-West* (London: Bodley Head, 1988), 149.

Bibliography

Robert, Clémentine. *Aldous Huxley: Exhumations: Correspondance inédite avec Sidney Schiff 1925-1937.* Paris: Didier, 1976.

Scott, J. D. *Vickers: A History.* London: Weidenfeld and Nicolson, 1962.

Sexton, James. "*Brave New World* and the Rationalization of Industry." *English Studies in Canada* 12 (1986): 424-436. Reprinted in *Critical Essays on Aldous Huxley,* edited by Jerome Meckier, 88-102. New York: G. K. Hall, 1996.

———. "Huxley's Lost Play, *Now More than Ever.*" *"Now More Than Ever": Proceedings of the Aldous Huxley Centenary Symposium Münster 1994,* edited by Bernfried Nugel, 57-81. Frankfurt am Main and New York: Peter Lang, 1995.

Shaplen, Robert. *Kreuger: Genius and Swindler.* London: Andre Deutsch, 1961.

Shaw, George Bernard. *The Intelligent Woman's Guide to Socialism and Capitalism.* London: Constable, 1928.

Sidnell, Michael J. *Dances of Death: The Group Theatre of London in the Thirties.* London: Faber and Faber, 1984.

Soloveytchik, George. *The Financier: The Life of Ivar Kreuger.* London: Peter Davies, 1933.

Sullivan, J. W. N. "Interviews With Great Scientists: VII—Aldous Huxley." *Observer* 1 (February 1931): 15-16.

Taylor, A. J. P. *Beaverbrook.* London: Hamish Hamilton, 1972.

———. *English History 1914-1945.* London: Oxford University Press, 1965.

Urwick, L. *The Meaning of Rationalisation.* London: Nisbet, 1929.

Vitoux, Pierre. "Aldous Huxley at Texas: A Checklist of Manuscripts." *Library Chronicle of the University of Texas* 9 (1978): 41-58.